THE MOB AND ME

THE MOB AND ME

WISE GUYS AND THE
WITNESS PROTECTION PROGRAM

FORMER U.S. MARSHAL
JOHN PARTINGTON
WITH FORMER ATTORNEY GENERAL
ARLENE VIOLET

GALLERY BOOKS

NEW YORK   LONDON   TORONTO   SYDNEY

Note: This work is a memoir. It reflects the author's present recollections of his experiences over a period of years. Some dialogue and events have been re-created from memory and, in some cases, have been compressed to convey the substance of what was said and what occurred.

Gallery Books
A Division of Simon & Schuster, Inc.
1230 Avenue of the Americas
New York, NY 10020

First Gallery Books hardcover edition September 2010

GALLERY BOOKS and colophon are trademarks of Simon & Schuster, Inc.

For information about special discounts for bulk purchases, please contact Simon & Schuster Special Sales at 1-866-506-1949 or business@simonandschuster.com.

The Simon & Schuster Speakers Bureau can bring authors to your live event. For more information or to book an event contact the Simon & Schuster Speakers Bureau at 1-866-248-3049 or visit our website at www.simonspeakers.com.

Designed by Renata Di Biase

Manufactured in the United States of America

10   9   8   7   6   5   4   3   2   1

Library of Congress Cataloging-in-Publication Data is available.

ISBN 978-1-4391-6769-4
ISBN 978-1-4391-6776-2 (ebook)

CONTENTS

CONTENTS

PROLOGUE

J udge Raymond Pettine was musing about the fact
that a top crime boss lived and plied his criminal trade
within a couple miles of the federal courthouse—an insult
to any good lawman, let alone Rhode Island's former U.S. attorney. My hippie mane recently shorn and our Caddy recently
borrowed, we were looking our best en route to T.F. Green Airport in Warwick, Rhode Island, to pick up Senator Robert Kennedy for the funeral of Congressman John E. Fogarty.

Pettine and I exchanged stories about the crime boss in question: Raymond Loreda Salvatore Patriarca, the son of Italian
immigrant parents. At the age of seventeen he was convicted for
breaking Prohibition laws in Connecticut. A series of convictions followed for such crimes as breaking and entering, white
slavery, and masterminding a jailbreak in which a prison guard
and a trustee were killed. By the age of thirty he had spent ten
years in jail.

Patriarca embodied the ethic of the Sicilian mob. Possessing
both brains and brawn, he drilled his crime associates with the
mantra: "In this thing of ours, your love of your mother and
father is one thing, your love for the Family is a different kind
of love."[1]

Patriarca also knew his way around politics. Despite being

---

1. Wiretap of Raymond Patriarca's office, circa 1966.

listed as Public Enemy Number 1, he served only seven months of a five-year prison term for robbery. An inquiry into his release revealed that the office of then-governor Charles Hurley had intervened and pushed for early parole. The parole was advocated by the governor because of a letter from a priest begging for leniency for the crime boss. The priest was a figment of the imagination of the governor's executive councilor, who was impeached when the ruse was discovered. Meanwhile, Patriarca came out of the probe with an enhanced reputation for his ability to reach into the governor's office. This wasn't the last time that Raymond Patriarca used the good graces of a "priest."

In one trial, a priest testified that Patriarca was with him attending a baptism in Connecticut at the time of a murder for which the crime boss was charged. Fortunately, the court recessed over the weekend, and Superintendent of State Police Colonel Walter Stone dispatched two troopers to the parish in question. There was no record of the baby or the priest over the preceding three years.

After one of his convictions, Patriarca broke out of jail, only to be subsequently recaptured, but it wasn't for naught: the head of New England organized crime, Phil Buccola, noticed Patriarca's toughness and management skills. When Buccola fled to Sicily in 1954 after having been charged for serious crimes, he ordained Patriarca the head of organized crime in New England.

Raymond Patriarca ruled with an iron hand. If his men made a mistake, they paid for it. When his men allowed a load of stolen cigarettes to be seized by the FBI, Patriarca made the bunglers repay him for lost profits. His empire spread to loan-sharking, gambling, hijacking, and extortion from businesses and the docks—nothing was unloaded from the New York City docks without "tribute" money being paid to Patriarca.

Patriarca ran his crime empire from a wood-frame two-story

building on Atwells Avenue (euphemistically known as the Hill, after Federal Hill, an Italian enclave in Providence) in Providence that housed the National Cigarette Service Company and Coin-O-Matic Distributors, a vending machine and pinball business. The street was like an armed camp: spotters were located everywhere so the Boss would have advance notice of visitors.

I had been sent by the U.S. Marshals to Patriarca's office in 1962 to serve him a subpoena. No sooner had I crossed the doorstep than two "made men" intercepted me. Raymond Patriarca was eating a slice of pizza and peered around the corner to see who the intruder was. As I reached for my badge inside my coat pocket, Patriarca dove back into his office, dropping the pizza on the floor. His bodyguards pinned me against the wall. They thought I was going to assassinate him.

"It's OK," I yelled, "I'm a federal man." The taller of the two guys nodded curtly at his partner, who pulled out my ID. Patriarca emerged from the back room and accepted an order to appear before a blue ribbon panel comprised of elite law enforcement personnel and politicians who were studying organized crime's influence on labor unions. His grimace told me that this didn't mean he wouldn't fight his appearance tooth and nail. He introduced me to mob etiquette: "Anytime you want me, kid, I'm here. Don't ever go to my house on Lancaster Street since I don't want my wife upset, *capise*?" He continued to read the subpoena while I stood there proudly, feeling like Eliot Ness.[2] Later, I learned that the FBI had a bug planted in the office. After

---

2. Eliot Ness was a hero of mine who died in 1957. He was famous for his efforts to enforce Prohibition in Chicago as the chief of the legendary lawmen unit known as the Untouchables because they were incorruptible. His team nailed Al Capone on income-tax evasion at Capone's illegal breweries. I wanted to be a Dudley-Do-Right myself and saw this subpoena delivery as one step closer to bringing another bad guy down.

I left, Patriarca called his attorney, Charles Curran, and intoned, "A goddamn *boy scout* just left after serving me with papers."

Alongside the FBI, the U.S Marshals had IRS agents watching who was going in and out of Patriarca's office. Hidden in a second-story apartment across the street, my team was snapping pictures of Patriarca, the people he spoke to, and the dealer plates on their vehicles. None of his "visitors" had real license plates, so the "borrowed" ones from auto dealers gave some leverage later to press the owner to give up the guy who had borrowed the plate on those rare occasions when we didn't recognize his mug. This was the way to gather intelligence as to who was in with the mob and who was on the outs. One bright day, Patriarca's guys spotted the sun reflecting off the camera lens. They stormed over to the building, cursing a blue streak. Mob guys never kill law enforcement personnel because they don't want the heat that a hit would precipitate. If words could kill, however, my colleagues and I would have been statistics. The jig was up—but my embarrassing incidents involving Patriarca were not.

Later, I was in charge of a detail recording the folks streaming into the El Morocco Club in Johnston, Rhode Island, for the wedding of Patriarca's nephew. I was filming away at a garage across the road while one of my guys was clicking pictures. After about an hour, some of the groomsmen noticed the glint from the sun on our lenses. Ordinarily used to the fact that law enforcement would make nonstop attempts to take pictures of the extended mob family (what better opportunity than a wedding or funeral?), the young turks obviously felt that we'd gone too far in impeding the happiness of the day. Rushing over in their tuxes, one of the hoods shouted, "Don't you guys have any respect?" Wanting to avoid further escalation, I folded up the operation. Besides, we had already captured enough information—or so I thought.

The following Monday I bragged to my superiors about the great filming I had done which showed various mobsters at the wedding. Confidently, I turned on the projector. The whole damn reel was blank. My face scarlet, I thanked God that my cohort's pictures had come out all right.

Bobby Kennedy emerged from the airport with a mane longer than my wife's. With a little chagrin over my recently axed hair, I greeted Kennedy. We started off toward the Cathedral of Saints Peter and Paul in Providence, but Kennedy was distracted. He told us he had to call his wife, Ethel. She was in trouble for "stealing" a starving horse from an adjoining property and feeding it. It was a cause célèbre in their state of Virginia.

As I learned was fairly typical behavior of the Kennedys, Bobby had no money for a phone call. We quickly detoured to the Howard Barracks on the property of the Adult Correctional Institution in Cranston, Rhode Island, for him to use a state police phone.

"Former attorney general and U.S. senator Bobby Kennedy is here to use the phone," I announced to the dispatcher and a few troopers within earshot. Because I had a reputation of being a kidder, they didn't believe me. Their mouths dropped when he came through the door and saluted them. They stood ramrod straight in formation and saluted him back. I was sorry that Pettine had stayed in the car, because he would have liked to have seen this moment of mutual respect.

Kennedy seemed in a lighter mood when he got back in the car. He quickly turned to the subject at hand as we gunned up Route 95 North. "How do we get that bum on the Hill?" He was referring to the fact that in 1959 the publicity-averse Patriarca had been forced to testify on Capitol Hill before the bright lights of the Senate Select Committee on Improper Activities in Labor and Management, known as the Rackets Committee. John F. Kennedy was a senator on the panel, Bobby its legal counsel.

During that hearing, Patriarca denied all knowledge of the Cosa Nostra or the Mafia. He sneered that the only mob he knew of was the Irish hoodlums, implicating Senator Kennedy's father. After Patriarca had concluded his testimony, he strode by the committee table and jibed, "Your sister has more brains than the two of you together"—a reference to the mentally challenged Rosemary Kennedy.

Bobby Kennedy had never forgotten the insult. Commentators credited the exchange with Kennedy's effort to eradicate the mob when he was attorney general. After Jimmy Hoffa made a wisecrack about the Kennedy men's affinity for Marilyn Monroe, Bobby went after him. He now had two related targets, Hoffa and Patriarca, whom Bobby thought were knee-deep into the coffers of Hoffa's union, the Teamsters. Bobby put together the first Organized Crime Unit (OCU) in the Justice Department despite FBI Director J. Edgar Hoover's insistence that the mob didn't exist. Kennedy selected Henry Peterson, Bill Lynch, then U.S. Attorney Raymond Pettine, and a host of others to form the OCU. Pettine became its prize prosecutor.

As I learned that day in the Caddy, the OCU's first meeting had gotten off to a bad start. Hoover was invited to Bobby's office for 1 P.M. The time came and went. Finally, the attorney general called Hoover's secretary, who announced that Hoover wouldn't leave his office. If there was to be any meeting at all, it had to be held on J. Edgar's turf. Bobby calmly threatened to have Hoover removed from his post if he didn't have his ass there in five minutes. Because Bobby's brother was the president, Hoover decided to comply. Later, I often thought back to this incident as a harbinger of the interagency wars that I would later confront.

As we approached the Cathedral of Saints Peter and Paul for Congressman Fogarty's Mass, the Witness Protection Program was born. Bobby was talking about Joe Valachi, who had decided to turn against the mob. Valachi was the key witness in 1963 during the televised McClellan Hearings into the rackets. He was a low-level guy and not particularly bright. He blew the whistle on the family structure of the mob, and he was significant because he was the first to violate "omertà," the sacrosanct code of silence among mob members. Valachi mistakenly thought that crime boss Vito Genovese wanted him whacked, so he decided to kill the hit man first. But Valachi killed the wrong guy and was caught. Facing life in prison, he decided to sing. Valachi served his reduced sentence in a protected section of prison.

Raymond Pettine had successfully prosecuted sixteen cases during his OCU days, but we all realized that new tools would be necessary now that the mob was catching on to Pettine's ingeniously hatched plots to nab his quarry. Moreover, a new program was needed, since there weren't many protected sections in jails for wannabe informants. Bobby Kennedy stated that the only way to catch upper-echelon organized-crime guys was to offer protection—freedom and a new life—in exchange for the conviction of mob bosses: "We need a guy with muscle to testify against his cronies. We got to get a guy who will finger the higher-ups and arm him with the protection of the United States government." He went on, "We can't treat him like he just broke into his first gas station to rob the till. We've got to protect him and his family from harm, give him a new identity, and a new start after he testifies against his mob bosses."

Shortly after our conversation on the way to the funeral, I was tapped to head the newly formed Witness Protection Program. My job was to guard the hoods and their families and make sure they stayed happy and alive so they would and could testify in court. The obstacles were many: not only was the care of gangsters with contracts on their lives a logistical nightmare, but law enforcement itself was a problem on too many occasions. For starters, it was difficult to know who to trust in the law enforcement community, since the mob had so many cops on its payroll. Who may or may not be an informant for the mob was a constant question when moving witnesses from one site to another.

As I began to be part of the wise guys' lives, I realized that these men had a code of honor. They weren't 100 percent bad. Like most of the people you will meet in this book, Raymond Patriarca had a good side. For example, when a boy in the neighborhood lost an eye, Patriarca made sure he had the country's best doctors and picked up the tab for the kid's care. Patriarca also dispensed money to widows and contributed generously to Holy Ghost Church, which serviced the Italian community on Federal Hill.

By the same token, while I worked with some sterling men in law enforcement, others fell short. When we didn't keep our word to the witnesses who risked their lives and those of their families, *we* became the bad guys. Some bureaucrats in D.C. didn't have a clue about life on the streets. Far too often they jeopardized the lives of the witnesses and us marshals who were guarding the witnesses. Stupidity and grandstanding also interfered with the functioning of the program.

In 1980 I testified before the Senate Permanent Subcommittee on Investigations to highlight both the successes and the breakdowns of the program. Generally speaking, the problems centered on the U.S. government's reneging on its own promises. This bad faith had to be rectified.

During my tenure I was responsible for the protection of over five hundred witnesses. By the time I left the program to become the U.S. marshal for Rhode Island, the program had eight hundred witnesses who made possible some 4,487 indictments with 3,071 convictions. For this book I have picked representative cases of the kinds of people we hid in places such as Miami, Long Island, Cape Cod, and Cumberland, Rhode Island. Many were bad guys who were surprisingly honorable, sometimes more so than my bosses in the program, who swore up and down that they would protect them after they testified and then would cut them loose over my objections. Other people I protected came from the right side of the tracks, but greed and the desire for power had turned them into common criminals. I have also talked about some women I had to protect, and they presented their own set of issues. Non-mob witnesses were pouring into the program during my waning tour of duty, including informants against drug lords. These witnesses were handled by another unit in the Witness Protection Program. The program grew too fast and encountered problems when the spigots were opened.

This book is the unvarnished truth about bad guys who were sometimes good and good guys who were sometimes bad. I'll always remember the lessons both taught—even those I wish I could forget. Some names have been changed to protect the innocent . . . and others to protect the guilty. For those who are still under protection, I've used their birth names and avoided their new identification. Seven of my charges who didn't follow our rules were eventually gunned down by the mob. The others may be living next door to you now.

1

THE BEGINNING

It was an awkward moment. Here I was sitting in the kitchen with a woman who was the antistereotype of a mob moll. Neither someone who eats a pound of spaghetti at lunch nor a bawdy babe, Claire Barboza was a little over five feet, with big brown eyes and light makeup, and weighed 105 pounds soaking wet. Fresh out of a Talbot's advertisement, she looked like any other housewife in this well-to-do Jewish neighborhood of Swampscott, Massachusetts.

She wasn't.

"What is expected of me, and what are you going to do?" she asked softly. Her arms were crossed as if to protect herself.

"I don't know," I shrugged.

No one had ever done this before, so I wasn't going to blow smoke. I knew that the mob had placed a $300,000 bounty on her husband. Joe "the Animal" Barboza had turned in his fellow mobsters. While he was safely locked up for the time being in a Cape Cod jail cell, it was this woman and their not-yet-three-year-old daughter who were most at risk. Federal and state indictments would be handed up against mob chieftain Raymond Patriarca and nearly a dozen of his crime-family members. The Animal was the star witness who could topple their empire. The important thing was the safety of his little girl. If the

Patriarca family killed her, Barboza would bury them, animated by revenge. But if they kidnapped Jackie, Barboza would never testify—he'd be sending his own child to the grave.

On cue with my thoughts, little Jackie walked into the kitchen. She was a Shirley Temple look-alike with her dark, curly hair and a bright smile. After about two seconds of shyness she climbed into my lap. She had a little cop in her with her rapid-fire questions: "Who are you? Why are you here? Do you like Oby my cat?"

Actually, I hated cats. Oby apparently could read my thoughts; at that moment the Siamese jumped on my lap. I brushed her off. Jackie started to bawl.

"You hate my cat! You hate my cat!" She and the cat ran off to another room. *Great*, I thought, *I'm certainly winning minds and hearts here*. At that moment I made up my mind to have a practice of always allowing pets to be under "protection" too. Pets would make the child's adjustment easier, but the animals would not be allowed to make public appearances other than for their "full constitutional," since a child's calling out the pet's name could be a link to the family's real identity.

I was trying to make small talk with Mrs. Barboza when the most god-awful sounds emanated from the next room. At first I thought there was another Barboza child crying in there and that my intelligence was incorrect about only one child. I asked if I could see what was happening; it was that cat crying like a child. Jackie started crying again, too, so I tried to comfort her. Just at that moment, one of the U.S. marshals stepped into the house to join me. Oby ran for freedom in what would be a precursor of his master's attempts later on. I directed the several marshals with me to retrieve the cat. Elite marshals dressed in suits and ties and police-issued black shoes were tromping around in the rain to the background wails of an inconsolable Jackie. We had been sent to fend off the most vicious mobsters in the world, and here we were, calling, "Kitty, Kitty, come back."

The marshals at first took umbrage that I had asked them to retrieve Oby. They didn't like to protect mobsters or their families, let alone a cat—they thought mobsters were scum. I would tell them, "What has Barboza's little girl ever done?" I knew it would be easier for the marshals to guard the Barbozas if they felt I cared enough to chase down the family cat.

Oby finally returned with a dead mouse and promptly deposited it at my feet. Claire Barboza shook her head and jabbed, "He's sending you a message."

When I told Claire Barboza that I didn't know what was next, that wasn't far from the truth. I had gotten my initial taste of protecting a witness in 1963. Eddy Choule was my "first muscle" in every sense of the term. He was a boxer and a middle-weight contender. He had an aura about him that he'd sooner punch your lights out than look at you. In exchange for immunity, Eddy agreed tentatively to turn against some mobsters in Brooklyn regarding a post office heist in which he was involved in Bergen County, New Jersey.

The major target of his testimony was to be Sonny West, a capo of the Gallo family.[1] The Gallo family ran the rackets, loan-sharking business, prostitution, and other vice activities in parts of New Jersey and Brooklyn. My job was to babysit Choule for three weeks and keep him in a good frame of mind so he could testify before a federal grand jury and later in court.

Our time together started off much hotter than the July weather. Choule was always looking for a way to get in a fight

---

1. A "capo" is an underboss who handles the details for the godfather of the mob family.

with me; I was never one to back down, either. He wanted to match up against me in weight lifting, a challenge I ignored. Would that I could have done the same thing when it came to chess: I played to win. One day he got so pissed off at me when I won that he challenged me to step outside and fight.

"Eddy," I said, "you know what we're here for. There's nothing to be gained." For some reason that calmed him, and we both sat down. I knew I couldn't resist trying to beat him at chess, so I decided I'd never play the game with him again.

My responsibilities went far beyond keeping Eddy alive to testify. The boxer continually threatened to back out of the deal. This dance of approach and avoidance about testifying was a very common occurrence. Uncle Sam was Uncle Sugar for many of these guys because of the free food, expense account, and attention. I spent a lot of time playing psychologist, stroking the witness, and inflating his ego (except when it came to chess!). I had learned a lot about stroking egos when I performed my military tour in the early fifties, and some of those skills came in handy with Eddy. I repeatedly reminded him of his grant of immunity and how he could start over from scratch.

One day Choule told me that he wanted to see his wife. He had been hotel-bound for ten days and wanted some conjugal rights. I thought it was a good idea; at least he wasn't asking for a prostitute. I called the U.S. marshal in charge, and relayed Eddy's request. I got the typical bureaucratic response: "It's your ass if anything goes wrong. You make the decision." He was the first of a long line of bureaucrats who were incapable of making any decision lest it ruin their career.

So I made the decision.

I told Eddy that the visit was a go, but there were strings attached. "Eddy, I'm going to set this up in Room 1107, a minisuite, for 6 P.M. with dinner delivered for the both of you. She'll be in room 711 and I'll accompany her to your room. By 7 A.M. sharp tomorrow morning you better knock on my door and tell me everything's cool, and you are still here." Eddy agreed.

At the appointed time, his wife went to the room. I left them alone; after all, this was his wife and I didn't want to chaperone. Nonetheless, I was like a father waiting for his daughter to come home from the prom. I walked back and forth in my room, never sleeping a wink. At 7 A.M. sharp I heard *knock knock knock*. My career was safe for another day.

Two days later Eddy asked if he could see his daughter. He wanted to go to church with his twelve-year-old. I acceded to his request. That Sunday, Eddy, his wife, and his daughter were in the pew at St. Francis Church with me in the row behind them. Eddy seemed to pray pretty fervently. We all went out to breakfast, and the love Eddy had for his daughter and she for him struck me.

When we got back to the hotel after the visit, Eddy had a surprise for me. "J.P., I'm not only going to give you the principals on the post office heist but also on twelve other crimes!" I was elated. Trying not to act too excited, I couldn't write down the info fast enough. This was gangbusters stuff. Eddy was giving me facts that would cramp the Gallo family for years to come. His information led to a dragnet of mob figures and a captain in the police department who was supplying guns to the mob. Somehow the captain managed to purloin uniforms so the crooks were able to dress as cops. Captain No-Good confessed to seven heists that he himself was involved in. He then led the Feds and me to a house where the mob stored its loot, including guns and hand grenades. It was one of the biggest mob busts in New York at the time. I received a call from Bobby Kennedy offering his personal congratulations. Eddy helped clear thirteen cases. Sometimes just being human with people will have results beyond what you could have dream.

On one of the raids, Choule warned me about a guy who

kept a live grenade in the second drawer of a bureau with the pin poised to release if the drawer was disturbed. Needless to say, without that information I would have pulled open the drawer and become confetti. Another time, we were playing cards until 2 A.M., when there was banging on the door. It turned out to be a drunk. One of the marshals, against regulations, had left his firearm out and Eddy went to retrieve it in case trouble was brewing. After I'd redirected the drunk away from the door, I turned around and saw Eddy holding the gun. Eddy nonchalantly went to the back bedroom and threw it on the marshal's bed.

Regrettably, back then there was no afterlife, no new identity or relocation for anybody who testified against the mob. Eddy dodged threats day in and day out. He'd pay a buck to somebody every time he had to start up his car in case it was rigged to blow up. Many months after his testimony, he called me about his son catching a bad beating.

Some months later Choule surprised me with a visit to my office in Rhode Island. He showed me a picture of his newborn son. "His name is John," he chuckled. I did the math. The baby was conceived at that conjugal visit.

So here I was, four years later, getting the job to be the architect of a program to protect the Eddy Choules of the world. The Barboza family was the first true test of the program. Joe Barboza was Bobby Kennedy's dream come true. At the age of thirty-four he had already spent half a lifetime in penal institutions, starting when he was twelve years old. He was a professional boxer for a while before he decided that he could make more money boxing the ears of those who owed money to a loan shark like himself. He reportedly fought in about five hundred fights as an amateur, a professional, and in the joint.

Barboza's reputation on the streets was folklore. One time he apparently ordered a sit-down meeting in a bar with a guy who was behind on his payments and was conning Barboza as to the reason. As the man continued to weave his yarn, Barboza did a Mike Tyson. He leaned over the table and calmly bit off a piece of the guy's ear. Another time he got into a beef with a Cape Cod police chief and killed the guy by tossing him into a lobster pit. The lobsters had him for lunch.

It wasn't long before Barboza was working for Raymond Patriarca. Barboza earned the nickname "The Animal" for very good reasons, not least of which was his execution of twenty-three people in hired murders at the behest of the mob. Raymond Patriarca knew how to make a buck off his bodyguard. When a bar owner complained to Patriarca that he needed protection from the Animal, Patriarca charged him a thousand dollars a month to keep Barboza away. He then dispatched Barboza to twenty nightclubs. Barboza roughed up patrons and broke furniture in bar fights. Several days after these incidents, Patriarca would send one of his boys to the same clubs to offer protection from Barboza. Barboza was a cash cow for the boss, though he was never a "made man" because he was Portuguese. That was fine with Barboza, since he had his own business of loan-sharking. At one time he had seventy-five guys collecting for him.

In 1966 Barboza was arrested in Boston on weapons charges. Bail was set at $100,000. The Animal expected to be bailed out by Patriarca. Instead, he cooled his heels in jail. Two of Barboza's pals shook down bookies and bars to raise the bail. The two friends were gunned down on Patriarca's orders and Patriarca pocketed the $70,000 they had raised.

Joe Barboza went ballistic. He couldn't believe that Patriarca had left him high and dry, certainly not after all the things he had done for him. Patriarca never completely trusted Barboza and considered him a loose cannon. "Someday we'll have to whack him," Patriarca would pronounce. He suspected that Barboza might try to muscle him out of power. Barboza learned fast that an assassin's bullet was waiting for him.

Like a jilted bride, Barboza was hell-bent on revenge. If he couldn't get Patriarca with his fists, he'd get him with his mouth.

While Barboza spent the spring of 1967 disclosing the dirty linen of the New England mob, I spent my time with Barboza's wife and child. Plans began to take shape for permanent protection before word got out regarding the secret indictments. I grew very fond of Barboza's daughter, Jackie. We had a routine. I would come into their living quarters every morning, and Jackie would be upstairs waiting. When she heard the door open, she'd call down from the second floor in her heavy Boston accent: "Jawn, is that you?"

Then I'd hear *click click click*, as she tromped down the stairs in her mother's high heels. She'd climb into my lap with the nursery rhymes she wanted me to read to her in one hand and Oby in the other. Thus began my workday.

As the team leader, I never got to go home. Other U.S. marshals came and went, but I was available 24/7. I sometimes had my wife, Helen, with me, which was a great adjustment for her. Years earlier she hadn't wanted me to become a state trooper like my brother, Billy, since troopers had to live in the police barracks six nights a week. I had acquiesced to her wishes and became a Cumberland police officer instead in 1955. Here we were, a decade later, and my job meant even more time away. Helen was as gracious as could be. She knew that this program was important and had to succeed, so she gave me leeway. I knew it wasn't exactly professional to involve my wife with Joe Barboza's family, but Mrs. Barboza needed a woman to talk to, and my wife was a great conversationalist. Also, I think my wife felt better being there since I was spending so much time guarding this great-looking woman.

Another reason I had my wife with me, particularly when Barboza was staying at the Cape Cod prison during his grand jury testimony, was that I didn't want any problems with accusations from him later on. Claire was young, dainty, and had a great sense of humor. I avoided any hint of impropriety by hiring Radcliffe College students as matrons round the clock when my wife wasn't there. I would sometimes bring my wife and son to the beach or amusement park with Claire and Jackie. I didn't want to be adopted as the new "man of the family."

Then word came down: the indictments would be unsealed. Barboza was joining us, and we had to leave to go into hiding with him.

As the appointed time drew closer for the Barboza reunion at a new safe house, Claire grew more restive. She wanted to go out on a Saturday night. Worse, she wanted to go to Revere, Massachusetts, to the Ebb Tide, which was a haven for wise guys. Mafiosi like Vinnie Teresa and Henry Tameleo, Patriarca's underboss in Providence, frequented the restaurant because the mob owned it. One thing that law enforcement had going was that unlike the Medellín drug cartel in Colombia, which had a "pop a cop" program for anybody who got in their way, the mob never took a hit at law enforcement except in a gun battle. It was bad for business, since any law enforcement official's execution would bring out the artillery. Also, the protocol of the mob was never to shoot where you eat. That too would be bad for business. Nonetheless, I tried to talk Claire out of the visit, but she was adamant, and I became concerned that she might fold before her husband ever returned. I made a calculated decision to grant her request since I knew that we'd be moving soon and that nothing would happen at the restaurant. Besides, it was important to signal to the wise guys that we weren't afraid of them. My marshals were all in place, with a couple of them babysitting Jackie. Some wise guys were in the restaurant when we arrived. One of my marshals stayed with the car to make sure the vehicle wasn't tampered with while we ate.

After dinner, Claire said she needed to talk to me alone. We went out to the boardwalk adjacent to the restaurant, and I knew something was amiss. She had had a couple of drinks, and so the questions came pouring out.

"All of this was make-believe," she said. "It's been peaceful without him. What's going to happen when it's over, John? What's going to happen when you leave? Where am I going to go, John?"

I realized that she was debating whether to leave Joe before the reunion. That would destroy the entire endeavor. Joe Barboza would never testify if she left him. I tried to comfort her. "Mrs. B," as I always called her, "The United States government is on your side." In my most reassuring voice I continued, "Don't worry about it. Uncle Sam will take care of you."

Claire wasn't convinced. "You don't know him, John. You think you do, but you don't."

I was about to find out just how right she was.

2

NEW ROOMMATE

I was sitting in a PBY, a Coast Guard seaplane that was like a flying Mack truck. I was en route that cold and foggy fall night to pick up Joe Barboza in Hyannis, Massachusetts. There were about thirty heavily armed state troopers on the tarmac when we landed. Barboza was standing in the middle of them. He looked like a gangster out of central casting. He was five feet eight inches of pure muscle, with a Jake LaMotta stance. It was midnight, yet he sported his signature wraparound sunglasses. A porkpie hat was perched on his caveman hair, and he wore a top-coat that was too long. Up close I saw he had a two- to three-day growth of beard with a bushy mustache that wouldn't quit. He was sucking an oval cigarette and blew smoke in my direction. I ignored it, thanked the police, and ordered him onto the plane.

"Jesus Christ, where's the rest of the guards?" he asked as he boarded the aircraft.

"I'm it, along with him," I said, pointing to Deputy Marshal Jack Brophy. Barboza swore again. "Put out your cigarette and put on your seat belt."

I saw his nicotine-stained fingers as he put the cigarette back into his mouth. "Put the cigarette out, put on your seat belt," he mimicked in a singsong voice. "What are you, a goddamn warden or something?"

I knew I had to establish control from day one, or Barboza would steamroll right over me. "Let's get this right," I said in an even tone, "I'm the good guy, and you are the bad guy. There's no in-between. You do as *I* say, or we'll sit in this fucking plane until morning."

Barboza took another minute then put out the cigarette and fastened the seat belt. Once we were airborne, Barboza asked me, "Are you Walsh?"—a reference to another marshal who had helped guard his family.

"I'm Partington."

"Oh, *you're* the prick" he snarled, immediately going on the offensive. "On the beach every day with my wife. The other marshals come and go. What's your goddamn angle?" I ignored him.

Barboza had heard that he and his family would be relocated to an island. His FBI guards, much to my chagrin, had been playing with his head. Like his wife, he had an idyllic image that was crushed as we touched down on barren Thacher's Island, off Cape Ann, Massachusetts. Barboza's mood grew even darker. There were no palm trees, just lots of poison ivy, rocks, and snakes. The snakes had been cultivated by the Coast Guard to keep boaters off. It was a great hideout, but Hawaii it was not. The FBI loved the hideout; visitors were rare, and escaping from the island would be like breaking out of Alcatraz because of the waves crashing against the shoreline. Landing a boat with assassins would be difficult for the same reason.

Barboza shook with rage. "My wife's gotta live in this shit place? My baby? Living here? What the hell are they going to do? You're bringing my baby out to this goddamn place?"

"It's either here or a ten-by-twelve-foot cell," I responded, though he did have a point about his wife and child.

Shortly after we landed, Barboza climbed up to the top of a rocky hill, a wide-open target for a sniper. I ordered him down.

I grabbed him by the leg. He sucker-punched me with a left hook, and I started to bleed. Just then two Fibbies (FBI agents) had landed by chopper and approached us. When they saw me bleeding, they laughed: "How's it going?" I looked over at Barboza. Assaulting a federal agent carried a ten-year jail sentence. He was bracing himself for trouble.

"Everything's okay," I responded. "No problem."

Something intangible happened at that moment. "Thanks for not ratting me out," he said as we headed to the cottage.

"I'm not a rat," I said.

"Yes you are, but you are a good rat," he pronounced.

That didn't mean that all competition between the two of us was finished. In the first few days everything was a challenge between us. I was a cop, he was a killer—we were natural enemies, a cat and a dog circling each other warily. Sometimes he'd take the offensive.

Sounding like Hannibal Lecter, he'd yell, "I'm gonna eat your liver." I had no doubt he would if he had the chance, and he'd wash it down with Chianti and a side order of fava beans.

"Joe, you don't fuckin' scare me, you know," I'd retort. I had a healthy respect for him, though—back him into a corner, and he'd make me number twenty-four on his hit list.

The house where Barboza and company would live was an old lighthouse built in 1861. There were two lighthouses, on Thacher Island known as the Twin Lights, both made of granite block and stucco. One was a working lighthouse that would automatically sound a foghorn twice every sixty seconds when fog enveloped the area, which was pretty regularly. The sound got on everybody's nerves. To say that the accommodations were rustic would be generous; the stucco lighthouses had fallen into disrepair as living quarters after the Coast Guard vacated the premises. Now bugs, rats, snakes, and seagulls inhabited the island, feeding off each other.

Barboza's "home" consisted of two bedrooms and two bathrooms. Our quarters were as weather-beaten as his were. With a dozen guys, we slept in bunks three to a room on a rotating basis and had an obsolete shower that operated from a catch basin when it rained outside. The furniture was junk. Blankets and sheets were in short supply when we first got there. It was always cold at night. There was no TV or phone for Barboza's use. It wasn't exactly home sweet home for anybody. In retrospect, Barboza got along pretty well with his wife, given the dire circumstances. I fought far more often with my lovely wife in a setting with all the amenities.

Here's how the detail worked. There were four posts: one was the lighthouse tower, with 162 steps to the top, from which the deputy on duty could see the entire island; the second was the perimeter of the island; the third post was around the quarters of Barboza and his family; the last post was at the rowing area, where boats could launch to shore or vice versa. Each shift was eight hours, and the men had to rotate every two hours so they wouldn't get too bored. Their posts require them to be alert to danger not only from without but also within. They were to make sure that Barboza didn't try to leave as well as watch for somebody who might get the draw on him. The island itself was a natural danger, with holes that a marshal could fall into and break his neck. Snakes patrolled the island. The men kept in constant contact with each other through walkie-talkies, and each post had field glasses. The men wore military clothing with military boots. The deputies held their post for a month at a time. Some of the marshals who rotated in had never seen the ocean before. One went fishing in the little craft we had. He threw over the anchor, but it wasn't attached to a rope to retrieve it.

At any given time there were twelve deputies (sometimes sixteen, depending on the danger alert) plus one matron and me watching Barboza and, more importantly, guarding against a hit. I felt bad for Claire. Here she was with thirteen men and no girlfriends to talk to, no place to go, and nothing to do. Things were even worse for Jackie. She had no playmates other than Oby, no swing set, no sandbox. We had to be hypervigilant for her safety because of the rough topography. One afternoon Jackie wanted to ride her bike. On these occasions I would accompany her, so there'd be no chance of her getting scooped up. Her father had told her "No," unbeknownst to me, and when she came and asked me, I said "Sure."

Jackie shouted with joy and jumped on her little tricycle. Barboza gave me a look that could kill. He grabbed her off the bike and ordered her to go into the house.

Jackie frowned at him. "I don't like you," she spat. "I want Jawn."

I felt terrible.

While Barboza hated us cops, the feeling was largely mutual. I knew I had to keep him occupied. For his wife's sanity, I couldn't have him with her every hour. Quite regularly the FBI would land on Thacher Island to debrief Joe. The Rhode Island State Police came to question him. I brought in a heavy boxing bag and a speed bag, which Joe would pound with a vengeance after his inquisitors had left.

The law enforcement brigade assigned to Barboza also seemed stir-crazy from time to time. They'd use any excuse to distract from the boredom. One afternoon somebody spotted a sea lion down by the dock.

"Let's catch it," one of the deputies proposed. They grabbed a rope, tied a noose on it, and went running to the dock.

"No," Barboza said, "let's kill it." He picked up a baseball bat and a butcher knife from the kitchen. Before long, Barboza had the rope and was carefully walking from rock to rock to ensnare the sea lion. As soon as he dropped the noose over the sea lion's nose, the animal reared back and knocked Joe into the ocean. The deputies roared with laughter.

"Hey, Joe," I said, as I retrieved the butcher knife from him, planning to find a new drawer for it. "What would it look like if that sea lion landed on you and you got killed? I can see the headlines: 'Barboza Killed by Sea Lion.'"

Joe scrambled back to dry land. "What if I got the god-damned noose around its neck and he dragged me across this water? 'Barboza Escapes with Sea Lion'! You asshole."

Joe started to collect a menagerie. He wanted a dog, so we got him a German shepherd. One time he tried to kill a seagull with rocks. He hit it, but it didn't die. When he spotted it limping, he nursed it back to health. Jackie wanted canaries, so we got the little girl two of them.

Barboza generally had a very soft side with his daughter, patiently teaching her the different colors or the letters of the alphabet. He spent hours combing her hair. Occasionally the family would invite me to dinner, and Barboza would lean over to his daughter and in the gentlest voice say, "Miss Jackie, show your manners, because John is here. You have good manners at the table when you have company. Be a good little lady." She would proudly comply.

As time went on the tension between us dissipated. We'd take late-night walks, sometimes at 2 or 3 A.M. Barboza would look up to the starry sky and sigh, "John, fucking what's up there? How important is it what we're doing here? We're so fuckin' small in the universe. We don't even exist."

I'd take some of these occasions to pick his brains. Who would the mob send to whack him? What would be the hit man's modus operandi? Would they kill a cop who was in the way? Joe, after all, was an expert in this field. He was teaching me his tricks as a mob hit man so I could keep him alive.

While late-night walks might paint a picture of tranquillity on the island, the situation was anything but serene. Danger was ever present. It took only about four weeks for word to leak out that Joe "the Animal" Barboza was stashed away on Thacher Island. One Boston newspaper's headline was "How to Hide a 250 Lb Canary."

One day we got a call that the wise guys had chartered a boat and had a sniper on board. Sure enough, after a few days the deputies spotted the boat off the island. I anticipated the hit by having everyone on the island dressed in the same clothing. I posted all twelve marshals and myself with our carbines in full view. I wanted the assassin team to think the island was an armed fortress. Even if they could have spotted Barboza, who was wearing marshal's clothing too, the water was too choppy to make the shot.

At other times when I used this same clothing ruse, Barboza would aggravate the heck out of me. He would, for example, insist on wearing a baseball cap backwards, just like he did on the streets. I would explain over and over again that this would make him a sitting duck. There would be the deputies with the cap brim in the front; Barboza's would point south.

The arrival of new deputies was an endless source of amusement for Joe Barboza. Anybody new would be met with a barrage of challenges. One young deputy, a kid named Joey DeRosa, was a former street kid who considered himself a toughie. This young kid seemed to be as hotheaded as Joe. I sensed an inevitable confrontation. A couple of days later, I decided that the three of us should take a walk together to ease the tension.

The two of them fell into a conversation about boxing. Barboza staked out a position that a great slugger like Marciano would always beat a good boxer.

"That's bullshit," the kid retorted. "Give me a good jab and I'll beat you." DeRosa had had a bit part in the boxing movie

Somebody Up There Likes Me, so his prowess might have gone to his head.

The next thing I knew, they were sparring. The kid threw a good shot and cracked Barboza in the face. Barboza never even blinked; he kept coming. He feinted to the right, then to the left, and threw a vicious right hook to the body. The kid was wearing a heavy parka, but it didn't matter: the X-rays showed three broken ribs.

Some deputies thought I was coddling Barboza because I got him boxing bags and would talk calmly to him when he was screaming, but I thought it was important to keep him happy. If it were just a question of keeping him safe, we could have stuck him in a jail as we had done during his grand jury stint. But there was more to it. Most people don't realize the shit that guys like Barboza go through once they decide to testify. Joe had been a criminal since the age of fourteen, and now he was going against his friends and becoming somebody he hated most—a rat. He'd be in hiding for the rest of his life.

Sometimes conditions got to me too. One night, after two months without television and too few diversions, I was playing cards with Barboza. He couldn't stand losing, so he said, "Whoever has the ace of hearts fucks his mother in the ass."

I was sick of him, his attitude, being on the island, and I was missing my family with a longing that wouldn't quit. I leaned forward, looked him right in the eye and said, "Joe, what if I told you I had the ace of hearts?"

Without flinching he said, "Then, John, you fuck your dead mother in the ass." I lunged at him. The other deputies had to separate us.

Later that night we made peace. We talked about how our lives might have gone had we made different choices. He was as cold as they come, he'd kill you in a heartbeat, but on the other hand, he wrote poetry and adored his daughter.

• • •

Right after word got out about Joe's hideout, Bob Morey, the chief marshal in charge, came up with an estate owned by millionaire John Babcock at Freshwater Cove near Gloucester. The digs were more to Joe's liking. The irony was that the new hiding place was right across the water from Cardinal Cushing's residence, which was full of nuns waiting on the cardinal. Joe would wave at them like an altar boy.

The move almost ended the detail. I spent the afternoon at the mansion unloading supplies from Thacher Island to set up the new operation. It wasn't like I could just load up a Ryder truck, so we marshals heaved everything back and forth by chopper, including the animals. Just as I was going to retrieve Joe and his family, fog set in, and the helicopter was grounded. The guards and Joe's family were all stranded with no food, no clothes, no heat, and no cigarettes. Without butts, Joe was mean.

I telephoned the deputy I had left in charge to advise him of the fog situation. We had tried to land a helicopter twice, but the effort was endangering the crew. Barboza demanded to speak to me.

"You really fucked this up but right," he growled. He continued like a schoolmaster lecturing an errant child. "John, I'm not going to blame you. But you fucking left me. You fucking left me. I'm going to tell you something. That fucking Morey. Take the message from me. I'm going to punch his fucking lights out. I'm going to punch his fucking lights out." Joe was screaming now, "He has no right! My baby! My baby is out here!" Robert F. Morey was the U.S. marshal for Massachusetts who had initially approved the use of Thacher Island. All Joe's resentment about this location came bubbling to the surface when he couldn't be relocated on this planned date.

I tried to talk Morey out of coming to Freshwater Cove for Joe's arrival the next morning. He had learned of the threat and decided to face Barboza before the situation really exploded. When the chopper landed, I saw Joe's face, and he looked like he was ready to pounce on Morey. As Claire stepped out, I grabbed Jackie from her arms and put her in Morey's arms. No way would Joe punch Morey now.

Later, Morey insisted on a private meeting. "Now Joseph," he said, "you have a very nice place here. You see this place you have here? It's a lot nicer than that Barnstable county jail, right? Now if you don't like it . . ." Morey's quiet, priestly voice suddenly rose, "Your ass can go down to Barnstable." Joe smiled; this guy Morey had balls. Joe took a step back with his palms facing Morey, as if to say *"Everything's cool."* Morey nodded and walked away.

3

FIRST TRIAL:
TREACHERY AMONG THIEVES

When Joe Barboza appeared before the grand jury in 1967, his testimony formed the basis for three separate criminal trials. Up first was the trial of Boston crime boss Gennaro "Jerry" Angiulo and his cohorts.

Angiulo was charged with being an accessory before the fact in murder and with conspiracy to murder. The target had been an ex-boxer, Rocco "Rocky" DiSeglio, who was the "finger man," the guy who chose the store, in a series of stickups of gambling houses in mob territory. Three other defendants on trial with Angiulo were accused of actually carrying out the hit. Rocco had apparently thought that he could rob these places that were under the protection of the Angiulo family with impunity. He was now pushing up daisies because he had figured wrong.

Barboza was brought into the courthouse under elaborate protection. There were four courtroom doors. Word had it that there were hit men monitoring each entrance whose job it was to stop Barboza before he sang. We smuggled Barboza into the Suffolk County Superior Courthouse at 2 A.M. on the first day of trial, January 10, 1968. Barboza and about twenty marshals all wore hoods with slits in the eyes so a would-be sniper could not fix on which one was Barboza. When transporting a witness to the grand jury or trial, a route was selected that would avoid one-way streets (the mob was notorious for using roadblocks for truck heists). A minimum of three inconspicuous vehicles were used for transport. At least one vehicle followed behind the one transporting the principal in order to provide protection from the back and side. Similarly, a vehicle in front was used to prevent frontal incursions.

All cars acted as backup vehicles in case of a mechanical failure of the principal's car, and each vehicle contained emergency medical equipment. On a case by case basis I'd decide whether we would need a police escort. If not, the transport crew was to obey all traffic controls except in an extreme emergency. Each vehicle was secured from a reputable car dealer and thoroughly searched for tracking or listening devices and, of course, explosives.

We varied the position of the principal's seat within the vehicle, but always with an eye to avoiding exposure to a drive-by hit. A lead vehicle could be several blocks or, in the case of a rural setting, several miles ahead, radioing information on a dedicated line. The route was scouted ahead of time to make sure that turns were right-hand only, in order to prevent a double block. As with all witnesses, Joe's departure from his residence was preceded by a deputy marshal's scan of the area with binoculars. Another member of the security force would examine the small ridges that surrounded the house and could have been used as a firing position. The advance vehicle patrolled the street immediately before departure to ensure that there were no hostile agents. Along the route, attention was given to houses and businesses.

Joe Barboza, like all principals, was given food and bottled water sufficient for his needs in order to prevent poisoning both en route and while he was in any uncontrolled facility. Even though his departure was in the wee hours, the protocol was strictly followed.

After Barboza was brought safely into the courthouse, he stripped out of his SWAT-team clothes. The trial's star witness was then cleaned up for his testimony: his once-wild mustache was pencil thin. His hair was slicked back. He sported a light-gray suit and dark tie. Barboza could look like either a caveman or a banker.

After being sworn in as a witness, Barboza sat on the stand jut-jawed. The prosecutor, John Pino, led Barboza through his story. In language larded with mobspeak, he testified that his partners in crime had murdered Rocco DiSeglio to save their own necks. Barboza said that it was put to the three defendants that they should either kill Rocco or be killed. The hit order came from Angiulo. Barboza said he knew about the scheme because he himself was present when the trio drove off with DiSeglio in East Boston on June 15, 1966.

Barboza recounted a conversation with one of the defendants the following day, when Bernard Zinna told him: "Joe, we did not go out on a score last night. We said that to set up Rocky. Rocky is dead." Barboza further testified that another defendant, Vinnie DeVincent, was with Zinna during the conversation and confirmed the hit. "I put a bullet in his head."

"I asked why," Barboza testified. "Zinna said, 'We were forced to do it. It was either him or us. Jerry made us do it.'" Putting the icing on the cake, Barboza went on to state that Zinna had confessed that it was the four of them who had robbed the gambling halls, and Zinna had told this to Angiulo, who had replied, "Either take care of him or I'll have all four of you taken care of."

Barboza testified that he went to Angiulo shortly after this conversation. They met at the Doghouse, another name for Angiulo's office in the north end of Boston, and Angiulo confirmed that he'd directed the hit.

Barboza said he tried to protect Angiulo by his visit because the executioners were mouthing off. He testified about his disgust for people who would do in a friend and said he'd warned Angiulo not to trust them.

He implicated the third defendant in the murder by recounting a conversation with him eight days after the slaying: Mario Lepore had allegedly told him that he had to go along with the hit even though he didn't want it to happen.

Procedural arguments then broke out, and the jury was escorted from the room. After their return, Barboza was on the stand for almost four days, most of that time being cross-examined. Barboza remained unshaken during his testimony but was damaged by the recitation of his long criminal record. Finally, he was asked whether he was the same Joe Barboza who had broken into a poultry store and stolen a rooster. Barboza looked disgusted.

"I don't remember stealing any rooster, Your Honor." The courtroom erupted in laughter.

The lawyers then taunted him about the book deal he was negotiating with Truman Capote. Defense counsel got him to acknowledge that he thought he'd be rich because of his book deal. The disclosure sent him into a rage. He quickly recovered, stating, "Nothing like that has motivated my actions against these men. There never would be a need for a book if these guys hadn't killed my friends."

Barboza answered no when asked if he had read *In Cold Blood*. The lawyer smiled, "You would like it."

The defense also mounted a counterargument that DiSeglio wasn't murdered in East Boston but in Topsfield. In his charge to the jury, the judge warned that if they did not believe Barboza and accepted the defendant's claim on the location, then they had to acquit. The defense hinted in closing arguments that Barboza was the real killer and also played on the fact that these defendants faced the electric chair on the word of a multiple killer.

The jury deliberated for less than two hours.

"Not guilty for all defendants." Angiulo bowed his head and cried. On the way out of court he paraphrased the time-tested radio remarks of the victorious prizefighter Rocky Graziano: "Well, I won, and I'll be right home, Mom."

Joe Barboza was going back to his marshal-protected home. The acquittal sent shock waves through the Justice Department. The jury hadn't believed Joe Barboza, who was also the chief weapon the government had against Patriarca, the next case up for trial. If there were no convictions, that would be the death of the program. The result weighed heavily on my mind. It bothered Barboza too: "See what ya get for trying to do the right thing?"

4

CHRISTMAS:
THE CALM BEFORE THE STORM

The long late-night walks continued on Freshwater Cove. Something like trust began to build between Barboza and me. One evening he began to talk about killing people.

"It's not like you see on TV," he said. "Like my first hit. I was with a partner, after this stooge. We're all set to do him in. We knock him down and he's out of it. Then I take my gun and start shooting until it's fucking empty. I see his eyes pop out, there's blood everywhere. It's unbelievable. Not everybody can kill. It's not easy. You can break kneecaps. You can punch people out. But to take a life, you know?" He didn't say this in a bragging or even a matter-of-fact way. He sounded like he didn't like it that he could push himself past an initial abhorrence to do the job.

Another time we were out late at night and he began to talk about a Russian Sputnik satellite that had just been launched. He wondered about whether there were such things as flying saucers. He thought that there was a strong probability of life on other planets. He would sometimes tell me stories that threw doubt on the existence of omertà, the silence oath. He would regale me with stories of wise guys who would drop a dime on one of their gang, squealing to the cops in order to get a promotion once the guy was out of the way.

Just before Thanksgiving I was leaving for a couple of days. I was going to take a mandatory physical and see my family. I missed them terribly. I knew that my wife, Helen, would still be speaking to me, but I wouldn't blame her if she didn't. I was tormented by thoughts that my son might have forgotten who I was. As hard as it was on me, I felt that I had placed a big burden on them with my absence. I was looking forward to the upcoming trials because when they were over, this detail would end. Barboza would go to another unit that would relocate the family and give them a new identity.

When I returned from a far-too-short respite with some guilt that the day was Thanksgiving and I wasn't spending it with my own family, Barboza pulled me aside. "John, where the fuck have you been? I missed you, you know? It's *our* detail here."

Then Barboza began to talk about the deputy I had put in charge. "You wanna know what the fuck that piece of shit said to me? He said, 'Joe, would you listen to me if Partington were taken off this detail?' Do you think bad guys are the only scumbags?"

"This is your brother." He jabbed his finger on my chest for effect. "You always call them 'brothers.' And he's kissing my ass, fixing my TV, wanting to know if I got enough food. This motherfucker was up in my room trying to make a deal with me. Well, I'm your brother, not him."

I knew I had to watch my back. This deputy whom I had put in charge hailed from North Carolina and had some political clout. With a little power, which I had given him, he became a bastard. In the two days I was gone, he had become number one on the walkie-talkie contacts. Joe had taught me to be cool although I was boiling mad at this usurpation, since the guy was a panty-ass. I remained cool and got rid of him when his tour ended. I didn't have to allow anybody to "re-up" for another tour, so when the guy sought another appointment, he was quite taken aback when I told him to climb the political ladder somewhere else.

Claire had taken Jackie to her parents' for the holiday. She must have had a fight with Barboza; he had scratches on his hands. After it got dark, I was completing my scan of the premises when something crossed my field of vision. It could have been a shadow, or it could have been someone crouched down and running across the courtyard. I went immediately to Joe's quarters. Empty. I began searching for him and found him in the main kitchen, which was outside his premises. He didn't belong there. He was standing by an open window, ready to jump out. I thought he was trying to escape.

"You motherfucker," Joe said quietly. Then he turned around, and I was shocked. He was foaming at the mouth. His eyes were big and black like a shark. I had suspected that his wife might have been bringing him pills, but I couldn't prove anything.

"What are you doing?" I asked. "You aren't allowed in here." At Freshwater Cove, there were four houses and a courtyard with a cobblestone rock garden in the middle. We didn't use two of the houses. Joe's family was in one house this time, with amenities like a television, and the deputies and I were in the other: again bunk-style, like in the military, with three bunks to a bedroom. The kitchen was used jointly, but Barboza wasn't supposed to be there without supervision. He was a great cook and often showed off his Portuguese cuisine for all of us. I allowed him to use a knife when he was cooking, which made some of the deputies nervous. I wondered where the blade was now, or the one I had taken off him in the sea lion caper.

"I wanted some food," he finally said, and began to calm

down. Then he walked within inches of me. "If you ever see me this way again, John, get the fuck away from me." He continued in a voice as cold as ice. "I'll fucking kill you. Don't you ever forget it."

Just a week before Christmas, Joe was taken to Boston to testify in a prehearing. Security was immense. Joe was extremely stressed and was swearing his head off at the smallest of provocations. It was the first time he'd be eyeball-to-eyeball with Raymond Patriarca, who was indicted on conspiracy to murder Providence bookmaker Willie Marfeo and on racketeering charges as a result of Joe's grand jury testimony.

While we were waiting in an anteroom before his testimony on a pretrial motion, Barboza asked me to do him a favor. "I gotta bring something back to Jackie, with it being Christmas soon and all. Get me a stuffed Santa Claus or something as a present." I dispatched a deputy to purchase a Santa. Joe then casually mentioned that he had the custom of buying a stuffed animal for his daughter after every hit. Symbolically, his testimony that day would be exactly that—a hit.

Joe walked into the courtroom and took the witness stand. Patriarca sat at the defense table in stony silence. As Barboza finished up his testimony, Patriarca made a fist, stuck out his thumb, brought it to the left side of his neck, and slowly dragged it across in a cutthroat gesture. Joe saw it, mumbled something about Patriarca's mother, and rose from his seat. Another deputy and I grabbed him before he could reach the godfather. His testimony was enough to bind Patriarca over for trial.

After Barboza's court appearance, we were going to return via a Coast Guard helicopter from the deck of one of its ships— it had its own landing pad. Otherwise, bogus applications for site landings at the initial and receiving sites would have been used to protect the "package."

Joe walked on the deck carrying this huge stuffed Santa, prompting some of the crew to laugh at him. Barboza couldn't stand it. "You motherfuckers wanna laugh at me? You want a fuckin' shank down your spine?" Stunned silence.

Once in the helicopter, Barboza announced that he had a present for me.

"You got me a present?" I asked with a fair amount of incredulity. "Where did you get it, Joe?" He handed me a fancy writing pad that even had a little light on it.

"Now you can write things down and remember them, Amnesia Head." He thought I was always forgetting things. Whenever he wanted something unreasonable, I'd stall him by telling him I forgot. It reached a point where he started calling me "Amnesia Head," since some of his requests were repetitive and I would try to ignore them. Joe grinned, and his voice got louder above the whir of the helicopter blades.

"I stole it off the first helicopter. I'm your fucking friend, John. I take care of you." He had held the "gift" from the very first time I transported him to Thacher Island!

Back at the safe house, we talked about putting up a Christmas tree. For practically all of the last seventeen years he'd been in and out of jail without any holiday celebrations, so Joe pined for a real Christmas tree. There were plenty of evergreens on Freshwater Cove but since the property belonged to the Coast Guard, it was a federal offense to take anything, including a tree. Nonetheless, I decided that we should chop one down. It would be great for little Jackie. Joe grabbed a hatchet and started to hack away at a pretty spruce. After about six whacks, he missed and hit his knee. Blood gushed out like a geyser. I could actually see yellow muscle. Another marshal and I got him to his quarters, where I poured pure alcohol on the gash and applied an adhesive bandage. Joe didn't blink a bit when the alcohol was applied. Nonetheless his injury was serious. It would have taken practically an act of Congress to bring a doctor to the mansion, since nobody was supposed to know who was there. Instead, we brought the mountain to Moses. A local doctor in town stitched him up pretty good and gave him a tetanus shot. Joe looked pretty respectable, since he had just been in court.

My friend, Dr. Robert Farrelly, used to perform most of the medical interventions but he was too far away to summon given Joe's condition. I trusted him like a brother. We had been best friends since the time we had raised our families next door to each other in Cumberland, Rhode Island. I was godfather to his sons, Bobby and Peter—the filmmakers of hits such as *There's Something About Mary* and *Me, Myself, & Irene*. Robert had his own practice as a general practitioner and worked pro bono for Uncle Sam. I would bring him in when emergencies arose and relied on him to provide medical histories for relocated witnesses that would be benign unless there was a true health problem, which he would then flag. Health "histories" had to be made up, for the protected witness and his family since the mob's "m.o." was to try to locate transplanted witnesses by paying off health claim personnel or forgiving debts of doctors who were gamblers if they traced the witnesses whereabouts. We'd often remark how these stone-cold killers were sometimes babies. Vinnie Teresa would almost faint at the sight of a needle. There were very few Barbozas who could stitch themselves up given enough malt whiskey.

One of the deputies must have reported this incident to Morey, who called me the next day to find out in his oblique way whether everything was okay.

"No problem," I said, and the conversation ended.

I don't want to literally make a "federal case" over a cut evergreen by putting Morey in the middle.

After the tree went up, it struck me how much the safe house looked like Bethlehem. Joe had picked up another German shepherd in Gloucester during one of our errands, so Olga and Otto were lying beside the tree. A stray cat that we had brought in from Thacher Island and Joe had adopted was now a sister to Oby. There were two canaries and a limping seagull. It was a downright menagerie.

The menagerie didn't last long. All the animals hated each other. Oby the cat ate the canaries before long. Harold, the newly acquired Doberman, eventually digested Oby, but not before the day when Joe got angry at the cat and tried to drown it by stuffing it into a sack and throwing it into the sea. Marshal Bud Warren heard the cat meowing while he was making his rounds; it was low tide and the sack had come back to shore. He rescued it. Barboza had a new respect for Oby, calling it a stand-up cat.

One day a stray dog wandered onto the property. Joe looked at the worn-out pads on the dog's feet and declared that the dog had been walking for two thousand miles. Joe wanted to test Otto, so he got them to fight. Otto circled his wannabe prey and pounced. The dog spun around and put his teeth on Otto's throat. Joe pulled the dog off and bit his ear. I never heard such a howl. Joe called him "Hobo."

Joe was also nuts about his second cat, Carrots. Joe would lock his room whenever he left, leaving the cat outside. But whenever he returned, the cat would be waiting inside the bedroom. Joe stayed awake for an entire twenty-four hours to see how the cat pulled this off. Apparently the cat climbed up the living room fireplace chimney and dumped out the connecting door to the fireplace in Joe's room.

The holiday mood was soon to change.

5

SECOND TRIAL:
THE GODFATHER'S TURN

Joe Barboza got more and more sullen as the time stretched out between the Angiulo fiasco and the upcoming Patriarca trial. I was getting pretty stir-crazy too. I missed my family. I had only one day off a month to see my wife and son during this fourteen-month stretch. I began to have doubts about the ultimate success of the program, particularly because the first jury apparently hadn't believed Barboza. On cross-examination, Barboza appeared to be a worse criminal than the people he was testifying against. If he failed against Patriarca, I felt it would be the swan song for the Witness Protection Program. The one hope was that the Angiulo trial, which was held in a state court, had been run differently from the federal forum where Patriarca's trial would be held. I had a nagging feeling, too, that the state court judge had given instructions to the jury that tilted the case in favor of Angiulo and company.

The mob boss's attorneys kept getting "continuances," buying time in the hope that Barboza would self-destruct. It wasn't a bad strategy—I had to work hard to keep him in a proper frame of mind. As the trial approached, the threat of a hit intensified. I ordered flares to be set up around the perimeter of our hideout.

If anyone approached the property, the flares would be tripped. One night, a seagull landed on one; flares shot up like it was the Bristol Fourth of July Celebration back in Rhode Island. The deputies ran toward the direction of the flares. I realized suddenly that Barboza was all by himself, so I ran back to his quarters. Barboza was standing guard, armed with the big kitchen knife.

"You fucking assholes! Whattaya doing? Leaving me alone?"

Joe didn't believe that it was a seagull. He thought that we'd captured a hit man. He constantly argued that the protection was Mickey Mouse anyway. He said that anybody could puncture our precautions, and threatened to prove it himself.

"Go ahead, Joe," I retorted. Damned if he didn't do it, just three days later. He snuck out of his quarters and crawled undetected into the Freshwater Cove compound, where he shouted, "See, you suckers?"

Meanwhile Patriarca's lawyers were trying to move the trial to New York City. The request for a change of venue failed. The trial was set for February 6, 1968.

Barboza had his own lawyer, an attorney named John Fitzgerald. He was receiving death threats. I urged him to accept full protection, but he just shrugged it off. He accepted bodyguards at his house at night, but wouldn't accept protection 24/7.

Fitzgerald was always careful when he started his car. Instead of getting into his vehicle and turning the key, he practiced a stunt he had seen in the movies. He would open the car door, stick one leg in and turn the ignition. Only then would he climb inside. His caution saved his life. On January 30, 1968, one week before the Patriarca trial was to commence, Fitzgerald went through his routine—only this time a round of dynamite was under the hood. It blew him out of the car before a second round engulfed his vehicle in flames. He lost his right leg right below the knee. The thirty-eight-year-old lawyer, a father of five, was using a car that Barboza had previously owned. There was some confusion as to who was the real target, but in any event, it sent a clear message. If Fitzgerald had accepted protection, one of my guys would have been injured or killed that night.

When Joe heard about the attempt on Fitzgerald's life, he threatened to go after Patriarca. I was concerned that he might try to escape, so I beefed up security. Joe tried to give us the slip but couldn't figure a way out this time. I asked him to renew his resolution to testify. It worked.

"Yeah," he said. "If I can't get that motherfucker with my bare hands, I'll get him with my mouth."

The judge postponed the trial until March 4 at the behest of the defense counsel. They argued successfully that there had been a barrage of negative publicity particularly following the car bomb that would affect their clients. Joe was really squirming to get the trial going. Finally, all the delays came to an end. It was showtime.

Getting Barboza safely in to testify was a top priority. Rumor had it that five hit men were stationed at various points to bump him off. Hours before the trial, Barboza was placed in a helicopter that landed near the Hatch Shell outdoor stage on the Charles River Esplanade in Boston. Eight men armed with rifles emerged from the chopper with Barboza in tow. A phalanx of tinted-windowed Cadillacs formed a motorcade to the federal Courthouse. My charge and I would live in a cell in the courthouse for three days during Joe's testimony, with bomb-sniffing dogs constantly on patrol. Everybody was on high alert. It was discovered that police uniforms were missing, so we had to guard against a thug dressed like a Boston cop. One of our detail found five hundred pounds of nitroglycerin that the mob had planned to throw onto the car carrying Barboza. Barboza exploded with laughter when he found out about this scheme. Surveying my five foot ten inch, 160-pound lank body, he declared, "Hey, J.P., that'd blow your bony ass right down to Providence."

On the second day of the trial, Joe was called to testify by prosecutor Paul Markham. Twelve federal marshals flanked the star witness as he entered the courtroom. Raymond Patriarca sat at the defense table charged with conspiracy to murder Willie Marfeo. His underboss, Henry "Skinny Man" Tameleo from Cranston, Rhode Island, was similarly charged, along with Ronald Cassesso, a Somerville, Massachusetts, punk, who was already in the can in Norfolk State Prison serving time for robbing an old lady a year earlier.

Patriarca parked his five foot seven inch, 160-pound frame firmly in the back of his chair. Upon Barboza's entrance he curled his body forward, planting two skinny arms on the table. His deeply lined face made him look like he'd been hired as an actor to play a mob boss. He wore a natty suit with a dark necktie and his trademark white socks peeking out from his polished brown wingtips. He looked bereft because he couldn't chainsmoke his trademark White Owl cigars.

It was the first arrest in twenty years for Raymond Patriarca, who had begun his racketeering career in the 1920s as a guard for some liquor hijackers—he made off with the liquor himself. He took over the top spot in the New England underworld replacing Frank "Butsey" Morelli after the other contender, Carlton O'Brien of West Warwick, Rhode Island, was ambushed by an unknown assailant in May 1952. He was anointed head by Philip Buccola, who fled the country in 1954 for Sicily rather than face racketeering charges that could have put him away for twenty large ones.

Barboza took the stand. He was an unindicted coconspirator in this murder. He described how Willie Marfeo, a small-time hood, had had the nerve to open up a gambling house a few blocks away from Patriarca's office. Patriarca and Tameleo told him to close. Willie pushed Tameleo and called him an "ass-hole." He shouted into Tameleo's face, "You people want a loaf of bread and you throw the crumbs back. Well, fuck you. I ain't closing down."

The Providence police paid Raymond a visit shortly thereafter. These cops told Raymond that the Marfeo operation was attracting too much interest. The brass at the police department would order raids all over Federal Hill if Marfeo's operation wasn't shut down. Raymond couldn't let that happen.

Barboza went on to testify that Patriarca and Tameleo sent for him and defendant Ronnie Cassesso. When Patriarca implied that he'd pay well for the job, Barboza said he'd do it for nothing.

Tameleo said, "I told you he was a good kid."

Patriarca replied, "I won't forget this, Joe."

Barboza explained how they planned to make the move on Marfeo. Raymond stated that he would supply everything, even a meat truck. Patriarca's idea was to use a meat truck with the killers dressed in white smocks with hats and pushing a dolly loaded with meat into the store.

"When we got to the sidewalk, we were to whack Willie." Barboza continued. "Henry [Tameleo] then showed us a couple of places Marfeo frequented."

After the meeting, Cassesso and Barboza got to talking. Cassesso was distrustful of Tameleo. He remembered a time that Tameleo had double-crossed a couple of guys who were doing a stickup by telling the cops, who shot the guys. Barboza decided to stall but testified that in the end he didn't have to initiate any delay—Raymond said the hit was off for a while because the law had heard about the beef between Marfeo and Tameleo.

Almost a year went by, and Barboza didn't hear anything. Then one day a low-level hood asked him if he had heard that Willie Marfeo had been slain in a phone booth. Barboza sought out Tameleo, who informed him that "we reached out for a good man." Patriarca said the hit man found Marfeo in a restaurant. All the customers in the building were Patriarca's people. The hit man took Willie out and over to the phone booth, where he was drilled with lead.

Because of the basic elements of this crime it was enough to prove the case of conspiracy to murder if the jury believed Barboza. The jury didn't have to believe the actual murder of Marfeo but had to believe there'd been an attempt to conspire to murder him.

The defense immediately pounced on Barboza.

"You intended to kill Marfeo in cold blood when you went to Providence, didn't you?" asked attorney Joseph Balliro, counsel for Tameleo.

"Yes," Barboza answered.

Balliro then covered the same ground he had covered in the prior Angiulo trial, getting Barboza to acknowledge his long criminal history and his book deal. He also elicited the fact that Barboza wouldn't be charged in this case if he testified against the others.

Barboza then left the stand. The defense decided to rest without calling any witnesses. Again the strategy was to let the case rise and fall on Barboza's credibility. In closing arguments the defense contended that Barboza's story hadn't been cor-roborated. In his summation the prosecutor argued: "Barboza's no angel, and the world would be a better place without the Joe Barbozas. But," he added, pointing at Raymond Patriarca, "if you didn't have the Raymond Patriarcas, you wouldn't have the Joe Barbozas. Who's worse? The fellow who opens the doors for the killers or the man who kills?"

Unlike the Angiulo trial, where the state court judge had largely granted the defense's request for jury instructions that I felt led to the acquittal, presiding justice Francis J. W. Ford instructed the jury that if they believed Barboza, then they had to come back with a guilty verdict.

Joe and I waited in the cell in the federal courthouse. After four hours of deliberations I was told that the jury had reached a verdict. This made me very nervous—usually such a brief time was bad for the prosecution. I went to the courtroom to find out the verdict.

Within moments I was back to Joe's cell. "Guilty, all counts!" I shouted. Joe started screaming like a madman, "We did it! We did it!"

All the time away from my family would have been for naught if Patriarca had walked. I had kept Barboza alive. Patriarca was taken down. The Witness Protection Program was made.

When we left the courthouse, decoy cars went first. I had to keep Barboza alive for a third trial. Joe was dressed in a marshal's uniform and he carried an unloaded M1 rifle to add to his disguise. He pretended to be guarding a real marshal named Jesse Gerder, who was pretending to be Joe. Barboza couldn't resist saying to Gerder, "All right Barboza, you asshole, keep moving," as we left the courtroom following Patriarca's conviction.

On March 25, 1968, Raymond Patriarca, the head of organized crime in New England, was sentenced to five years in federal prison and fined $10,000. Tameleo got three to five years and a $10,000 fine. Cassesso got five years and a $10,000 fine. The Witness Protection Program was looking good.

After I got Joe Barboza settled back at Freshwater Cove, my boss directed me to deliver Raymond Patriarca to Atlanta to begin his incarceration. This was almost a year after his sentence because of Patriarca's appeals. The mob boss was about to see the "goddamn Boy Scout" again. Patriarca had seen me accompanying Barboza into the courtroom to testify against him. I wondered how he'd react to my switching to "companion services" for him. Gerry Ouimette, one of Patriarca's stable, was now rumored to be trying to take Patriarca out in order to get a fast promotion to top boss. My transfer of Patriarca would be anything but routine.

I was aware that the marshals guarding him had treated Raymond Patriarca with extraordinary deference. It was standard operating procedure to handcuff the prisoner and put leg irons on him when taking him to and from court. They had not done so, out of some misguided respect for the don. When I got to the holding cell, I ordered the marshal with me to shackle Patriarca. The mob boss shouted in protest. He then got in my face.

Screaming in protest at the top of his lungs, the boss got to me. I called him an inappropriate name.

"I'll have you like a goddamn bug," he said, snapping his fingers at me.

I brought him out to a waiting police vehicle. We had a brief skirmish, probably due to the fact that he had a hard time maneuvering with the leg irons on. He fell into the car screaming invectives at me.

En route he chewed my ass, telling me that I had no respect for my elders and that my father was a stand-up guy. I had no idea how he knew my father, who was a construction worker. Of course he was right. I apologized sincerely. That calmed him down a bit.

We finally got to T. F. Green Airport with our heavily armed contingent and boarded the plane after it had been searched. We sat where marshals always sat with prisoners—in the first row of coach, behind first class. Within moments the chief pilot came out of the cockpit and motioned to me. I got up to talk to him.

"Is that Raymond Patriarca?" he asked, jutting his jaw

toward the mob chieftain, who was wearing handcuffs. He already knew the answer since I had to declare on paper that I was a U.S. deputy marshal who had a firearm on board. I nodded yes.

"I'm very nervous with him on board," the pilot replied.

"Don't be, you gotta fly the plane," I responded.

Raymond Patriarca watched the exchange with amusement and then called out. "Hey, Captain, c'mere a minute." Meekly, the pilot obeyed. "I wanna smoke, is that okay with you?" Patriarca reached into his pocket and pulled out a White Owl cigar. Legend had it that he wore white socks to match the band. I knew otherwise. He wore white socks because he had diabetes. Cotton socks kept the feet dry, so a sore would not develop. Raymond would also be able to tell if he was getting an infection from wound pressure because he'd see the blood on his white socks and prevent further ulceration.

"Certainly, Mr. Patriarca," the pilot said. "Let me light that for you." He pulled out a lighter but thought better of getting too close. He handed the lighter to me. In those days smokers had to sit in the back of the plane, but Raymond was allowed to smoke in the nonsmoking section. Effusively, the pilot offered us first-class seats, which Patriarca quickly accepted. I nixed them. Then we were off to Atlanta.

We chatted easily on the plane. He brought up our first meeting, when I served him the subpoena. He was pretty relaxed for a guy going to the pen.

When we got to Atlanta, they let us off the plane first, and there was a law enforcement team waiting to escort him to jail. My job was to deliver him safe and sound into their company, but he asked me to ride with him to the prison. I did. This invitation was tantamount to his bestowing an honor on me and his way of letting me know that bygones would be bygones. En route I met another marshal, Murph the Surf, a maverick James

Bond type. He hopped into our car, and it was like three guys going to a Red Sox game. Eventually, we arrived, and I said goodbye to the Man. Patriarca nodded and went off to Processing. I knew this wasn't going to be the last of him. He'd soon prove me right.

6

THIRD TRIAL:
HENRY TAMELEO TIMES TWO

In between the trials, Bobby Kennedy was assassinated. I was bereft that I hadn't been there to protect him. I felt remorseful about his death and also because Bobby Kennedy had asked my superiors to allow me to guard him in Chicago at the 1968 Democratic National Convention should he be the Democratic presidential nominee. I already fancied myself as his protector and rued the lost opportunity perhaps to have saved him. My head told me that I would not have made a difference, but my heart wanted the chance to try, and then to celebrate my friend's triumph when he got the nomination. Joe Barboza was so upset about the assassination that he went into seclusion. This made me wonder what made Barboza tick, since he'd been responsible for at least a score of hits on unsuspecting guys.

New deputies came to guard Joe. Most were good guys who went with the flow. Others were prima donnas or were just plain incompetent. One marshal got into a beef with Joe. I felt the deputy had provoked the argument so he could get off the detail—I obliged him. Another time a half-asleep deputy dropped his gun. This fellow's rifle shot went through the wall. Joe Barboza hit the deck before anybody. I was furious.

"I don't know who the hell you know, asshole, but you have one minute to get outta here or your ass is grass!" I yelled. I realized I was over the edge. To manage stress, you have to eat and sleep right, two activities I had been neglecting for months.

Around this time one of the deputies, Lee Colson from Minnesota, was guarding Barboza. He wasn't responding to a walkie-talkie communication, so I sent somebody to his post. He couldn't be stirred. Following protocol, I called Bob Morey the Massachusetts Marshal as we rushed him to the hospital. By the time we got to Massachusetts General Hospital, Lee had passed away. He had a massive brain hemorrhage. I hated having to break the news over the phone to his wife back home. She let out a low wail, and my heart broke for her. A doctor got on the line and told the wife that there was a donor card on his person. She agreed to the donation of his organs. Later that night his body was flown home with an honor guard of four from the service.

When Joe Barboza found out, he was genuinely sad. He had gotten along with Lee. Getting a death-related pension for one's family was extremely difficult at that time; it was granted only for those who died while actually on duty. Barboza came to the rescue. He told the investigator who came to interview everybody that he saw Lee die at his post, since he wanted Lee's family to get the service-related pension.

"I saw him trip and fall, and he whacked his head on the side of the building." The Colson family got his pension. Barboza's mission was accomplished. I was a bit dubious as to Joe's version, but I wasn't a witness, and I wanted the widow and the children to get the pension.

The third and final trial for Barboza involved Henry Tameleo, Patriarca's underboss, and five others. They were all charged with the gangland slaying of Edward "Teddy" Deegan, a high-ranking member of the Charlestown Mob. Deegan was murdered as a result of a modern-day Hatfield and McCoy blood feud between two Irish gangs, the Charlestown Mob and the Winter Hill Gang. Initially the war started because one wise guy dissed a rival gang member's girlfriend. The war over turf between these factions accounted for at least fifty dead, and the number was more likely closer to one hundred. Raymond Patriarca originally sat out the war, figuring that the warring "micks" as he called them would kill each other off. He finally decided to back the Winter Hill Gang because of his 20 percent cut of the gang's take from loan-sharking, rackets, protection money, and heists.

Barboza had emerged as the family's top triggerman in March 1965. He had accepted a $7,500 contract to kill Deegan. Barboza recruited several partners to help carry out the hit. Eventually, Deegan caught two in the back of his head that ripped apart his brain. Although Joe would subsequently testify that he hadn't pulled the trigger, he was the lookout in the Chelsea Massachusetts, alley where the execution had occurred. Other defendants emptied their bullets into Deegan's body as well, according to Barboza.

On June 27, 1968, in advance of his testimony in the third trial, Barboza pled guilty to conspiracy to murder. Because of threats on Barboza's life, Judge Felix Forte cleared the courtroom of the press and the public and ordered the doors locked in advance of Barboza's plea. The previous month, Barboza had pled guilty to charges of conspiracy to commit murder of Anthony Stathopoulos, a pal of Deegan's. Barboza's sentencing was postponed until after his testimony in the Deegan trial. Stathopoulos was also in protective custody when he decided to join the program and testify against his former buddies after an attempt on his life. He had been at the scene of the Deegan murder as the driver of the getaway car during what he supposed to be a bank burglary. When he heard the gunshots, he drove away before he was snuffed out since he was supposed to be shot, too.

The trial was set for July 1 and proved to be the most contentious of the three trials. Again I had to resort to a repertoire of tricks to keep Barboza alive long enough to testify. In the courtroom itself, the judge had all the shades drawn on one side of the courtroom to prevent a sniper from taking Joe out from a perch on one of the nearby buildings. Police dogs were on duty, and everybody was searched before entering the courtroom.

I was regularly informed about the schemes used by the mob to get Joe. They were pretty creative. One man from a Chicago crime syndicate was brought to Boston. He got himself arrested as a drunk and locked up in the basement of the courthouse—all to determine if there was a way to get to Barboza and kill him in the building. His subsequent report: "Mission impossible."

Barboza arrived in court in a green sports jacket and chinos. He dropped his voice occasionally, prompting the judge to urge him to speak up. I noticed that Joe didn't look at the defendants during his questioning, which was unusual given his eyeballing of the defendants in the first two trials. He began his testimony by claiming that he had visited one of the defendants, Peter J. Limone, in his "doghouse" (office).

"I said 'Here is your bread,' and handed him some money."

"What was the money for?" Assistant District Attorney Jack Zalkind inquired.

"Interest on the vigorish [loan] I owed him."

Barboza said that Limone walked outside with him and told him that he had $7,500 and it was his if he killed Deegan or arranged for somebody else to bump Deegan off. The mob hated Deegan because he was a braggadocio, trying to impress them with the murder of Anthony Sacramone, whose bullet-riddled body was found in his car in 1964. The bodies of two other hoods associated with Deegan had been fished out of Boston Harbor; they had hit the home of a bookmaker who was protected because he had paid his tribute money. The Cosa Nostra wanted Deegan dead because he swindled the organization and made a show out of everything.

Barboza testified that told Limone he wanted to meet with Tameleo before agreeing to the hit. Tameleo confirmed that Deegan had to go. Barboza made the arrangements and then collected his $7,500. He testified that he was congratulated for "a good piece of work." "The Office [Cosa Nostra] was pleased," Tameleo told him. He later divvied up the $7,500 with the other defendants on trial.

The cross-examination commenced right after the Fourth of July holiday. Occasionally Joe'd give flip answers. When a defense counsel tried to get him to change his testimony about the slaying, he quipped, "I was there, you wasn't."

At one point, one of the defense counsel was using a chart of the murder scene and placing pins at strategic spots. He scornfully asked Barboza to tell him where to put one of the pins. Barboza retorted, "You want me to tell you what you can do with that pin?" The spectators howled with laughter.

When another defense lawyer got in his face, Joe told him to back off. He looked up plaintively to the judge, "That guy has bad breath."

Once a defense lawyer complained that the prosecutor was trying to signal Barboza about what to say. That brought a barrage of angry denials. The defense counsel tried to bait him by asking him to agree that he was the biggest murderer in Massachusetts. The judge did not allow an answer.

At another time during the trial, the defense accused the judge of having a double standard, one for the prosecution and another for the defense. I thought this was a desperate tactic. The defense counsel was hoping the judge would loosen up on some rulings if it looked like the defense could claim bias on appeal. The judge would have none of it, commanding the defense lawyer to "Sit down!"

Barboza remained cool as a cucumber until the third day, when a defense lawyer asked him about his wife wanting to leave him in 1965 because of his girlfriend. Love letters to another woman—not his wife—were introduced. Joe at first had amnesia about them but later agreed they were his missives. Barboza was obviously taken aback by the line of questioning, since mob guys aren't supposed to talk about another guy's *comare*, or mistress. But omertà was out the window now because they were fighting for their lives. Knowing Joe, I could imagine him going into damage-control mode with his wife, who would find this public recitation very humiliating.

Yet another defense counsel revisited Joe's testimony that he was told by Tameleo that he'd done a good job. "You want this jury to believe that you were told 'you did a hell of a job last night' by the defendant, is that correct?"

"Yes"

"But [Deegan] was supposed to be shot inside the hallway."

"Yes."

"So, it wasn't a good job was it?"

Barboza answered dryly, "He's dead, though."

Barboza was also questioned about his failure to see who actually shot whom. He acknowledged that fact, though he testified that he knew what went down because he was the foreman and manager of the plot. Barboza's crime streak was used against him again, as well as his big book deal. After five days of testimony, Joe was beginning to shout at the defense counsel. Even the judge had to shout a few times to be heard during the wrangling. At one point, defendant Limone's lawyer accused Barboza of concocting this story against six innocent men so he could live with his wife and child.

"You want the jury to believe your story to help convict these men," the attorney stormed.

Barboza shrugged his shoulders, "I don't care."

The seven days on the witness stand were making their mark. The courtroom was stifling hot, and not just because it was a July day. After nine days, Barboza retired from the stand. He stated on redirect testimony by the prosecution that he believed that the mob was trying to kill his family after killing his friends and that was the motive behind his informing on his prior gang associates.

Finally the trial, which bordered on a resemblance to the Barnum and Bailey circus, came to an end. It remained to be seen whether the jury panel would consider Joe a P. T. Barnum, who believed there was a fool—like them—born every minute, or a witness who was telling the truth despite his checkered past. The jury was out for quite a while. Joe was exhausted.

The jury returned its verdict some eleven days after the state rested its case. All six men were found guilty. Eventually four defendants, Tameleo, Louis Greco, Peter Limone, and Ronnie Casesso, were sentenced to death. Two others Wilfred Roy French and Joseph Salvati, each got life without parole. Joe was happy. I was elated for the Witness Protection Program. Of the three trials he testified at, two ended in guilty verdicts, four members of the gang were sent to death row, two to life in prison, and Patriarca was tucked away in the Atlanta Penitentiary.

Barboza returned to court on November 1, 1968 to get his medicine for being part of the Deegan death. A detail of heavily armed U.S. marshals brought Barboza to the courthouse. The Boston police met us in the garage. Other officers, including from the FBI, guarded the fifteenth floor and its approaches. The judge noted that U.S. Attorney Paul Markham had credited Barboza with being the key figure in the successful prosecution of the Cosa Nostra of New England. The judge sentenced him to a year and a day for his part in the Deegan murder. The sentence was to run concurrently with the remaining year Barboza was doing as a result of the gun charges that had led to his arrest prior to his cooperation. At the request of the prosecutor, while Barboza could be free after the remaining year, habitual criminal charges were filed against him. Were he to return to a life of crime, the charges could be reactivated and would carry a sentence of life imprisonment. Joe thundered a big "Thank you, Your Honor." After all, it was better than the eighty-three years he could have been sentenced to.

Now that the testimony was all over, it was time for Joe to move on. Later, this entire case would be revisited. For now, though, it was time for me to transition Joe out of the program. That would take some doing.

The Witness Protection Program is quite accurately described as a high-threat program predominantly designed to get bad guys to testify against worse bad guys. At its heart, however, it is a serious relocation program. The for-life protection requires a permanent identification change for every family member and the obliteration of all ties with that family's past community. When a witness goes underground, the family is debriefed by a psychologist. The psychologist asks very probing questions to ascertain what the risk is to the community contemplated for the relocation. The shrink's role is also to predict the kind of antisocial behavior likely to accompany the moving of the family. Family photographs are ditched, and no direct contact is allowed with extended family or friends. Nowadays, there is also an orientation center where the families attend sessions lasting several days. The family does not know where the site is, since they are transported in bulletproof vehicles with blackout curtains.

The orientation center is an area within an area. A patrol guards the perimeter. The inside is surrounded by a barrier under constant surveillance. Inside and out, electronic surveillance and anti-intrusion systems are on 24/7. Vocational inventories are administered to the protected witness to gauge job aptitude, final "certified" documents of the new identities are provided and a cover story is made up and rehearsed. Nowadays, all paperwork has a judicial trail whereby true identification records are recorded and sealed in the District of Columbia federal court. Earlier, as in the DC federal court case of Joe Barboza, the redocumentation was "pocket litter." The end product was the same: the original person ceased to exist.

Barboza and I had been together for sixteen months, longer than a lot of marriages. The detail was about to wind down, and Joe was an unhappy camper. He was boiling angry. He had spent months on the front pages of the news. He'd grown used to his elegant digs on Freshwater Cove. Now he was to be transitioned into Phase Two. He'd be given a new name, relocated, and cut loose from my aspect of the program. He didn't take to sayonara.

"You're gonna see the real Joe Barboza, not the rat fink," he growled, when I explained that he had to move on from the safe house.

"Bring your shiny badge. Bring your shiny gun. Because you're going to need them."

On a frosty morning in 1968, I had to take Barboza to the airport. I suspected that his threat was real and that he wouldn't go without a fight. I decided against a show of force, because there could have been a bloodbath. I counted on Joe having some empathy for me since the two of us had gone through a lot together.

I called over the marshal whom I trusted the most. "I'm going in there alone," I told him. "There" was the hotel room where we had stashed Barboza prior to his flight. "I'm going to take the walkie-talkie. If I click twice, you have a round in that carbine because you're going to have to shoot. You understand me? Can you do it?"

The marshal nodded; I knocked and let myself into Barboza's

room. He was coiled for action. Joe hadn't shaved. His baseball cap was on backwards. His Rocky Marciano muscles were bulging through a white T-shirt. I'd seen that look before. He was primed for battle.

I casually strolled over to the couch, clutching the walkie-talkie in my right hand. I stretched out and pulled my own cap lazily over my eyes. I acted like I didn't have a care in the world.

"Joe, we'll leave here in ten minutes," I said quietly. Barboza was speechless. Where was the cavalry to take away the great Joe Barboza?

He started to open his mouth, but I cut him off. "Joe, do you think for one minute, after all you've done, after all *we've* done, that it could end in a showdown? We've gone through too much together. I'll tell you what we're going to do. We're going out the way we came in. Just you and I. No leg irons, no handcuffs, just you and I."

Barboza understood that he was being offered a gracious way out.

"No handcuffs? No leg irons? Just you and me?"

I nodded. He peered out the door, expecting to see an army of cops outside, maybe to waste him. He spotted only the other marshal.

"Hey, Joe, how's it going?" the marshal asked.

"Get the car," I directed my partner. "Everything's okay. No problem."

Joe got into the car with his two German shepherds. When we arrived at our destination, he put on his wraparound shades and came up to me. "See ya, Amnesia Head. By the way, I left you a parting gift in the apartment." He walked away. It turned out to be Hobo the dog.

I watched Joe get on the seaplane and take a window seat. He glanced at me and smiled. Pulling out a cigarette, he drew on it long and hard. I remembered our first tango over the cigarette. He was telling me, *Fuck you, Partington, you didn't change me a bit*.

As Joe's plane took off, my marshal buddy turned to me. "You know what, J.P.? The only bad thing about the detail? He's gonna get up there, he's gonna open that door on the plane, throw those two dogs out, and leap out and escape. And you're gonna hear them say: Joe Barboza escapes out of aircraft making some derogatory remark about somebody's mother."

I broke into unstoppable laughter. I actually started to tear up from laughing so loud. It was as if air were let out of a balloon, I was so full of pressure. Sixteen long months, away from my family, on three or four hours of sleep a night. When the going got tough, I had stayed because of his little daughter, Jackie. The program had worked just like Bobby Kennedy and I had believed it would: a witness with muscle had brought down the mob.

Joe's plane was no longer in view. I was heading to my family for a little R & R in Cumberland, but first I had one more job to do. I had to help Claire and Jackie pack and then transport them to the Army post at Fort Knox, Kentucky, where Joe would be finishing out his sentence in one of the barracks. Joe had attracted so much notoriety during his trials that a prison wasn't a safe environment for him.

No sooner had I parked my bag in the living room and kissed my wife like there was no tomorrow than the phone was ringing. Helen gave me an "Oh, no" look. Her instinct was right on target. I was being summoned to Boston to put out a forest fire. Claire was balking at joining Joe at Fort Knox. She was pregnant, and the marriage was on the brink of breaking up. The pressure of the trial had been an enormous strain on their relationship, and the introduction of the love letters at the Deegan trial had pushed Claire over the edge.

"Honey," I said, trying to smooth things over with *my* wife.

"I have to leave but I will make it up to you, I promise." She smiled, but her eyes were telling me that she thought maybe I was P. T. Barnum after all.

All the way to Boston I invented several scenarios of how I would make it up to Helen. *She has the patience of Job*, I thought as I fought my impatience with Claire. I wanted to go into her room, ask her "Whatddaya want?" answer her, and beat it back home, but my head told me I'd be talking with Claire for a long time.

Upon arrival, I still had an edge of impatience. "What's up, Claire?" I began. Claire was in a small hotel in downtown Boston. I did a lot of talking, and she did a lot of sobbing. I finally convinced her to join Joe at least for a little while for the sake of Jackie. I promised to visit them in a few weeks to check up on them. She reluctantly agreed.

I was in for a tough transition. I had become in a sense a bit of a wise guy myself. Over the sixteen months, I had internalized a take-no-prisoners approach. After all, if I could handle Barboza, I could handle anything. Not long after the detail, I received the Department of Justice's top award for service. I took Helen to the ceremony, kissed her good-bye, and then went alone to Roanoke, Virginia, for a training session set up by the new director of the U.S. Marshals, a former military general with political contacts. All the guys from the Barboza detail were there, and it turned into a celebratory party. I was introduced to the general.

"So you're John Partington," he said in his most pompous voice. "Well, I'll tell you what. We're going to start handling these punks and these wise guys the way they *should be* handled, *not* the way *you* handled them. Put that in your little book. The road ahead is not the road you went on."

At first I was speechless. I was proud of the Barboza detail and all that had been accomplished. Here was this military beanbrain berating me. I looked at my boss and said, "You must know a lot about the military since you're wearing all those fucking stars. But you don't know a fucking thing about wise guys or about men. You don't know anything." It was his turn to be stunned. Later on I found out that it was his two fair-haired boys I had thrown off the detail. I felt mighty good mouthing off at him. I sounded, well, like Joe Barboza.

The first few months of relocation are very tough on a witness and his family. Being thrown together more than they would be in a "normal" household wreaks havoc, since the couple is used to being apart or at least having an artificial them-against-us togetherness while under protection. Old skeletons come out of the closet, and resentments pour out of the spouse, who often hadn't previously known of her husband's real occupation. Spouses and kids miss their former life, family, and friends. Adjusting to a new identity is wearying, since there is so much tension being out in society. The Department of Justice initially wasn't doing a very good job at relocating witnesses permanently. Joe Barboza was given at least two new identities. His daughter had to be rehearsed all over again. "What if a stranger asks you your name? What if they ask you where you come from? What if they ask you this or that?" Usually the mobster has no problem lying—it's in his bones. For the wife and child, however, it's an ordeal. Claire was being driven crazy by being asked questions about her accent, and making new friends was a trial, lest she be discovered for who she was. Exchanging confidences with a new girlfriend was out of the question. The fear of the unknown can be very severe.

After a few calls from a frantic Claire, I kept my promise and visited her, Jackie, and Joe Baron at Fort Knox, where he was finishing his sentence for prior crimes not covered under the immunity agreement (he wouldn't be prosecuted for any crime he acknowledged during his testimony). The marriage seemed a little better, but the full pressure was still off, since he was in the slammer.

I learned a lot from my experience with Joe. I never really *liked* him but had something bordering on respect once he began to testify. It wasn't easy being a snitch; it went against the very grain of the hit man. His family paid a dear price. The simplest of tasks became complicated. Jackie had to get school transcripts to enroll in school. She had to unlearn her last name. Usually children keep their first name since it's hard for them to remember two names. Getting an apartment or a loan became very difficult without a credit history. Job references were unavailable.

After doing his time, Joe sent me a postcard from a cruise to China. I wondered how he could have afforded the trip, and it sure wasn't going to be because he had a job that paid him a mint. I harbored the thought that Joe was back to his old ways. One night I got a phone call. It was Joe, and he wanted to see me in Seekonk, Massachusetts, on the Rhode Island border. I was livid. Part of his deal was that he was never to come back to New England. He begged me to meet him at midnight at a Howard Johnson's restaurant. I parked so I could see all the traffic coming in and out of the lot. At the stroke of midnight, Barboza arrived with his traditional shades on and a submariner's hat. There were two gals and a guy in his Avis rental car.

"Follow me, John," he requested.

"Naw, you get in my car." He did, and the other car followed us. I know what you are thinking. It wasn't the brightest thing to do, but I was going on instinct that he wouldn't hurt me. We drove to a pizza place. His cohorts were trained like marshals, hovering over him while we ate. He really had nothing to say except small talk. He told me he was doing some ad hoc carpentry jobs. I left him on 295 North in Massachusetts along with my admonition that he get out of New England. As he drove by, he leaned on the horn and tossed me the finger.

I realized the next day why he had paid this impromptu visit. A guy called Jesus was killed in Massachusetts around the time Joe was with me. Joe wanted me as his alibi. To this day I don't know what part, if any, Joe played in that murder, but I'm sure it was connected with his trip.

About four months later I got a desperate call from Joe when he was in the Berkshires. Apparently, he was still turning a deaf ear to his parole condition that he live outside of New England. The Barboza (now Baron) family was living together 24/7.

"She's leaving me," Joe said. I drove up to see if I could patch things up, but the marriage was on a resuscitator. Unlike in the past, when Claire had to stay with Joe to protect herself and her child, there was no longer an upside, since the protection had come to a halt. She had the experience of being safe with her new identity under her belt. I had no leverage to keep her in the marriage, nor did I want to do so when I saw that she was just worn-out. She now had a second child, a son, with Joe, and I sensed she did not want the boy to absorb Joe's hardness. I realized that this marriage could no longer be patched up. In fact, it had been on borrowed time back in the days on Thacher Island. I explained to Joe that there was nothing I could do.

It was the last time I'd see Barboza alive.

I well remember the date, February 11, 1976, when I received a call telling me that Joe Barboza had paid the price for testifying against his former gang members as he was walking to his car. A white van was seen fleeing from the scene, a quiet residential street where Barboza, now known as Bentley, was slain. He had told me, "There's one thing in this game. Either you kill me or I'm going to kill you. You don't live long in this business." It had come full circle for him.

Barboza was one of seven witnesses out of five hundred I had guarded who left the program and thought they could make it on their own. I subsequently learned that the government had set up Barboza and his family in Santa Rosa, California, under the name of Joseph Bentley and put him in cooking school. Barboza had something else cooking, though. At the time he met me in Seekonk, he had flown in from California using Uncle Sam's stipend in order to meet with the Boston Mafia to negotiate a payment in exchange for his recantation in the Deegan case. Apparently, he wasn't offered enough money!

Subsequently, there were gun charges and in 1971 a murder conviction over stolen securities. We could take Joe out of the mob but we couldn't take the mob out of Joe.

In 1985 the world learned who had slain Barboza. According to James N. Chalmas, Barboza/Baron/Bentley was his roommate after Baron left prison in 1975. Later that year, Chalmas met with Joseph (J.R.) Russo, who had orders to kill Barboza for his testimony against Raymond Patriarca. Ironically, Chalmas testified in October 1985 against Angiulo in a federal court. Whereas Barboza's earlier testimony hadn't convicted Angiulo in the first trial, now Barboza's death stood to do precisely that. Angiulo and capo Larry Baione a.k.a. Ilario Zannino were on trial for conspiracy to kill Barboza.

Under a grant of immunity, Chalmas testified as to how Barboza was set up for the kill by J. R. Russo. The FBI was wiretapping Angiulo's headquarters five years after the slaying and caught Angiulo making corroborative statements reliving the hit on Joe. The trial lasted about ninety days. In the end, all of the defendants were convicted of clipping Barboza. Their own bragging convicted them. Joe got the last word after all.

• • •

In subsequent years it was thought by some that the FBI had withheld evidence regarding the Deegan murder. In a letter in 1974 to his then girlfriend, Barboza appeared to mock his Deegan testimony. After more than three decades of prison mornings, Joseph Salvati and codefendant Peter J. Limone had their convictions in the Deegan case overturned because a judge concluded that the FBI had withheld reports suggesting that Barboza had lied to the jury. An investigation ensued into the Boston FBI's relationship with the Winter Hill Gang's fugitive boss, James "Whitey" Bulger, who is still on the lam and faces charges of killing nineteen people. Salvati's lawyer, Victor Garo, contends that Barboza implicated an innocent Salvati to cover for his balding buddy and fellow hit man Vincent Flemmi, a.k.a. Jimmy the Bear. Meanwhile, codefendants Greco and Tameleo died in prison, and Salvati and Limone spent three decades behind bars. This case came up again and ensnared an FBI agent named John Connolly, who initially served a ten-year sentence. Connolly was convicted of protecting two organized-crime kingpins, one of whom was Whitey Bulger.

In July 2007 the FBI was whacked with a $102 million penalty in a lawsuit by the defendants' families in a stinging rebuke for withholding evidence that would have exonerated the defendants—not the least of which was proof that the FBI knew Joe Barboza had lied during the trial. The federal Judge, Nancy Gertner, concluded that the FBI had also encouraged Barboza to lie and that two other FBI agents handling the Deegan murder claimed to have corroborated Barboza's story when they could not. It appeared also that FBI agent Connolly had let Joe get away with the murder to protect his Boston source and longtime friend, Whitey Bulger, by wiping out the competition.

The recent vindication of the defendants stands as an

indictment of the coziness between Boston mobsters and the FBI agents. Apparently, Barboza had seen a way to ingratiate himself with the FBI by going along with framing the wrong perpetrators while helping his pal, hit man Jimmy Flemmi escape prosecution for the Deegan murder. The evidence suggested that Barboza had committed the murder with help from Flemmi, who had turned out to be an FBI informant. The information on this murder surfaced in 2001 in the form of FBI memos discovered during a probe of Connolly and other Boston FBI agents' complicity with gangsters Stephen "the Rifleman" Flemmi (Jimmy's brother) and Bulger, who has been on the FBI's Most Wanted list for a decade.

Ultimately, Connolly got an additional life sentence in a 2008 trial on state charges for fingering World Jai Alai president John Callahan as the informant and soon-to-be witness against Bulger in the murder of Roger Wheeler, the owner of a jai alai fronton. This experience was not only a black eye for the FBI but also a big blow to the Witness Protection Program, notwithstanding the fact that no marshal was implicated in any wrongdoing. Marshals have to have a sense that the person they are guarding—not to mention for whom they are risking their lives—is at least performing a public service against bigger dirtbags. I, at least, had always rationalized my misgivings about protecting murderers by convincing myself that this was the only way to catch worse offenders. When I realized from the episode involving Connolly's earlier wrongdoing that I couldn't trust our partners in the FBI and the Justice Department, I began to feel a bit jaded. The FBI is supposedly looking for Bulger, but I wonder about how sincere that effort is, since his capture would probably unearth other "bodies" and scandals for the Fibbies. I had to redirect my anger and skepticism by focusing on the innocent family members—the children and spouses—so I could do my job.

A final postscript on the Barboza matter: One day I got a very tearful phone call from Jackie, Barboza's daughter, who was then in college. She often sent me letters, and I responded to each of them. This day, she required an eyeball-to-eyeball meeting. She sobbed immediately when she saw me.

"Why didn't you tell me, John, what a bad man my father was?" she asked through a bucket of tears. It seemed that she had taken a course on organized crime and her professor had referred to Joe Barboza as a true animal, like his nickname. The professor flashed Joe's picture up on the screen, and Jackie froze. I told her that I held back so she'd have a father-daughter relationship and not be poisoned by hate. Jackie had thought of her father as a hero and that he and I were on the same side. She had become a law enforcement major so she could follow this path herself.

She said she understood why I was silent all these years, but when she left our meeting, she was still heartbroken. I think I did the right thing in not telling her, but I'm not sure.

Joe's son, who was conceived while Joe was in witness protection, turned out to be a great kid. He saw the truth about his father on a syndicated TV show called *Top Cop*, which centered on the Witness Protection Program and Barboza. I also met with him and smoothed things over, or so I hoped. I was struck by the fact that both of Barboza's children were majoring in law enforcement.

Three years later I received an invitation to Jackie's wedding. Claire was there. She was still beautiful and sat in the front pew with a gentleman whom I assumed was her companion. I decided not to ask later, even though I was curious, because I thought my query might be misconstrued. We had always acted appropriately with each other, but I had picked up vibes that she might have wanted our relationship to be something else. On the other hand, maybe I'm just flattering myself by thinking so. I was very proud of the bride, a newly minted graduate who was about to join a law enforcement agency. I slipped into the pew moments before she started down the aisle. She smiled at me and I grinned back. As she passed me, I turned my attention to her groom. I was somewhat taken aback—he looked just like Joe Barboza!

Oh, my God! I hope looks will be all they will ever have in common.

8

BANKING ON IT

Upon the conclusion of my assignment to protect Barboza, the Witness Protection Program really took off. Previously, the only way a mob guy would get out of the Mafia was in a coffin by natural causes or at the receiving end of a barrage of bullets or other form of sudden death. Barboza's protection—despite the $300,000 hit contract—changed this dynamic. The wise guys who wanted to get out were beginning to believe that the government could protect them and their families.

Almost immediately I was quarterbacking half a dozen new entrants into the system. This number would grow into hundreds during my tenure. While I no longer spent 24/7 with them, I nonetheless spent considerable time with each witness to gauge his (and sometimes her) needs and those of the families. I was responsible for coming up with a plan of protection until the court trials in which each was to testify were concluded, deploying the necessary security, and turning them over to the next phase of the process with a new identity, a new location, and sometimes a job.

Some of these guys had an affinity for banks. One of the new entrants into the program was Vincent Charles Teresa, better known as "Fat Vinnie" because he tipped the scales in excess of

350 pounds. Newspaper reports would estimate his weight anywhere from 250 pounds to 450 pounds. I should know—I spent 95 percent of his time in protection with him and I saw him taking up two seats on a plane.

Vinnie had refused to become a made man, although he had grown up as a child with a Mafia dad. For twenty-eight years he worked on behalf of Raymond Patriarca as well as for himself and other gangsters. He was a near genius. His schemes victimized a lot of so-called legitimate people. For example, he'd promise a doctor or other professional a huge return on an investment of, say, $70,000. Dr. Pure-Heart would be told that the investment would be laundered through the mob, but where else could he get a 25 percent return in three weeks? Greedy doctors and professionals would shovel money his way. Fat Vinnie would keep 30 percent for himself and turn the rest over to Raymond. When the investors came looking for their returns, Vinnie would shrug and tell them that Raymond appreciated their donation. What could they do? He knew they couldn't go to the cops to complain that they were supporting the mob and making money off the books, and they were afraid of Raymond—so they got stiffed.

Vinnie redirected the mob into more upscale crime. His schemes included bank swindles. He'd get a name off a tombstone and secure a loan from a credit union for his "friend," a recently arrived Italian immigrant, using the deceased's name. The paperwork was nonexistent. The loan officer knew of his contact with Raymond, so he'd fork over the money on a handshake, usually because of fear. It was a shakedown. The immigrants distrusted the police and were worried about their legal status in the country, so they didn't blow the whistle, while Patriarca got the money. Even when the banker required an application beyond the name for the purpose of the "books," such as they were, Teresa would fill it out with phony information. The lender was still porked, since he hadn't done any due diligence to determine the bona fides of the borrower. Again, Teresa would give 70 percent to Patriarca and keep 30 percent for himself.

Cashing phony checks was another part of Teresa's repertoire. He and his gang would first cash a legit money order to see how the inner workings of a certain financial institution operated. Using an old printer, Teresa would then make up batches of checks from various companies and sign the signatures of the owners with a check-writing machine. He'd select a name out of the phone book as the payee and create a phony driver's license. He'd hit a different section of a state with bum checks on the same day, selecting area banks, supermarkets, and small grocery stores. He kept the checks in the $120-to-$150 range because most of the time the teller could cash such a check without asking the manager. Of course, Teresa already knew what banks would require the involvement of a manager, since he'd already tested the system with legitimate money orders first. He expanded this scheme from Massachusetts to Rhode Island, Connecticut, and New York and made tens of thousands of dollars. Later, Teresa would joke to me that he should have been given a consultant's fee, since his machinations finally got banks to shape up their check-cashing procedures.

Teresa also fabricated drivers' licenses for a fee. In one coup, he rolled up his shirt and reported to the Registry Division of Licensing in Massachusetts. "Gee, I'm new here," he professed to an innocent-looking ingenue. "My boss sent me to pick up a box of licenses. Can you tell me what floor they are on?" The young lady dutifully sent him upstairs. He spotted the nameplate of the guy sitting at the front desk and said he was there to see Eddy Pick. "That's me," the man replied.

"I've been sent up top to pick up that box of new licenses," Teresa said.

"Oh, sure," the civil servant replied without so much as a glance at Teresa. "They're over there in the corner." With a forged rubber stamp of the state seal, Teresa and company sold a thousand forged licenses for fifty bucks a piece, keeping some back for the check-cashing scheme.

Soon Teresa preferred life behind the teller's cage: he expanded his repertoire to bank robberies. Why travel around when you can pick up a bundle in one hit? He was involved in four bank robberies, one of which got him pinched, along with a swindle of a bank in Lynn, Massachusetts, whose manager wasn't quite so intimidated by the Patriarca name. This turn of events eventually brought Vinnie to my doorstep.

Vinnie had actually come to my attention before this, though. He had participated in trying to hit Joe Barboza on Thacher Island. He rented a yacht and brought a couple of assassins on board to plug Barboza until our show of force and the swelling waves foiled the plot. Of course, that didn't stop Teresa from claiming that he had me in his rifle sight.

The FBI was piling charges on Teresa from other swindles because his victims were emboldened by the example of the brave branch manager in Lynn. Vinnie was willing to take his knocks, but only up to a point. At Lewisberg Penitentiary, where he was awaiting trial, Teresa was living the life of Riley. There was a "Mafia row" that housed almost four hundred Italians. The place was kept in check by Joe Bananas (Giuseppe Bonanno of the New York mob) and *capo di tutti capi* Carmine "Cigar" Galante, who managed to smoke cigars in his prison cell and who ran the wing in this who's who of top mobsters, reporting only major problems to Bonanno. Prisoners got plain buttons on their uniforms. Teresa's had pearl buttons. Long sleeves were mandatory. Teresa hated long sleeves, so he was the only inmate in short sleeves. Because there was such order under Galante, the unit was awarded with privileges. Italian food would blanket tables in the cube-shaped wing as family members brought in pizza, pasta, calamari, veal pizzaiola, and chicken cacciatore. It was a sweet life if you had to be in prison.

The outside mob, however, did something unforgivable in Teresa's eyes. Taking care of the inmate's family was sacrosanct, particularly for somebody like Teresa, who claimed he had provided $150 million to the mob while "earning" only $10 million for himself. Blanche, his wife, received nada to support herself and their three children. One visiting day she informed Vinnie that she hadn't received a dime, not even a penny for Christmas. Blanche had been to see one of the underbosses, who blew her off by saying he had problems of his own.

Another disappointment for Vinnie came with the indictment of his son, Wayne, on perjury. The underboss, Joe Black, had apparently promised a lawyer to represent the kid. On the day of the trial, no lawyer showed up. You might be wondering why Teresa didn't just hire a lawyer. First, it was a question of honor. The mob was supposed to protect its own. Second, he was an inveterate gambler. He'd lost everything on the ponies.

Teresa's son was convicted.

When the FBI visited Vinnie to see if he would talk following these indignities, his name was announced over the loudspeaker to report to the front office. This worried him, since a visit to the front office meant that law enforcement was there to see a prisoner. By design or not, the visit shook up Teresa, who began to worry about protecting his back inside the pen.

The straw that broke the camel's back was another visit from Teresa's wife. She was frightened as she told Vinnie that a big black car had driven up next to their daughter, Cindy, when she was walking with a friend. "Get in," she was ordered. Cindy screamed and bolted with her friend. It's an open question to me whether this was mob-related or law enforcement putting on the squeeze through pretense.

Vinnie decided to talk.

Because of the threat of his being murdered once the word got out that he was cooperating, Vinnie was moved from the Lewisberg federal penitentiary to the Baltimore County Detention Center in Towson, Maryland.

While he was in the Maryland facility, the FBI visited frequently with Teresa. I wasn't yet involved with him. I was off in other parts of the country, processing other informants, but I got word after a short time that Vinnie was holding back on information; it was time for an FBI squeeze play. The decision was made to put him on trial for the Lynn Bank and Trust swindle for which he had gotten busted.

The FBI told him that they couldn't do anything because it was to be a state trial. In fact, he hadn't been forthright with them, so they were returning the favor. The trial involved a tombstone loan for a "friend," the money from which Vinnie had used for loan-sharking. The case was airtight. Vinnie agreed to plead guilty and asked his wife to contact the FBI for more talks. His sentence was postponed as he sang like a canary in exchange for the promise of protection and reduction in jail time. By the time Teresa was through, out of around fifty indictments, thirty-two organized crime figures would be convicted in nineteen different trials.

In 1971 Teresa came under the protection of my marshals and me, since his odyssey to testify in trials against his former pals was about to begin. He had a detail of nine marshals because then attorney general John Mitchell had called me to impart information about particular threats on Teresa's life. I took Teresa out of La Tuna Federal Penitentiary in El Paso, where he had been moved by the FBI, to John F. Kennedy Airport in New York. We boarded an Allegheny Airlines plane headed to Rhode Island. Upon arrival, I stashed him at the Holiday Inn at the foot of Federal Hill, near the wise guys, because they would never expect him to be under their noses.

To say we didn't hit it off is an understatement. Initially, Teresa didn't want anything to do with me, since I was from Rhode Island. He scornfully informed me that we were all tied to the mob. When we arrived at the Holiday Inn at 11:30 P.M., he was certain that I was behind some plan to get him rubbed out. A screaming match ensued. At one point I told him, "Wanna go outside and swim in the pool, asshole?" He reluctantly backed down.

The next day I brought him to the Homestead Air Reserve Base in Florida. He loved the facility, since he got to live in the presidential headquarters. His wife was going to join him, but not before she stopped to testify to a Providence grand jury about her contacts with the mob while Vinnie was in jail. Vinnie didn't have much time for a reunion, since I had to take him to Baltimore the next day for another case, *United States v. Mastratro*. This traveling back and forth was grueling for him and our detail. He'd be in D.C. and Boston within the space of a couple of days to testify. He had a heart problem and high blood pressure and one time forgot his pills. It took some doing to get a prescription for a nonexistent person—in the end a pseudonym pulled us through.

Teresa never stayed in the same place; we'd move each night because he was such a high-risk target. One time we'd be in a Holiday Inn in New Hampshire, another night in a hotel in Attleboro. Finally, the whole family was reunited in a safe house in Smithfield, Rhode Island. The safe house was like a fortress: electric sensors ringed the yard, the windows were alarmed, the control room was filled with electronic gear.

Teresa started off as a constant complainer. The Fibbies had indulged his every whim. I laid down the law, and he eventually acquiesced, although I did show him some respect by consulting him on his safety plan.

Vinnie got to dress in regular clothes even though he was technically a prisoner serving his sentence with us. He fancied himself a clotheshorse. He was Mr. Casual, wearing loose clothes because of his girth. He'd wear open-collared polo shirts with plaid pants and a checkered jacket. I didn't care what he wore, as long as he was ready to testify.

Vinnie told me how to spot a mobster on a plane: "He's the guy who looks like he's snoozing—he doesn't want to talk to you. Check his nails. If they're manicured and polished and his shoes have a shine, he's one of us. His shoes will always match his socks. His overcoat will be the same material as his suit. He's wearing money."

What usually kept Vinnie in the proper mood was food. He was a double-upper. At breakfast he'd down one or two dozen donuts. He always had at least two dinner entrées and desserts. He'd devour a family pupu platter on his own—he was nuts about Chinese food. He'd down Pepsi unremittingly; I knew we were breaking the ice when he asked me in his deep gravelly voice if I wanted some soda from his supply.

There were aspects of his crime life he didn't like. "I went to too many goddamn funerals of guys who were close to me," he'd moan. "It was so hypocritical. Guys would be saying how sorry they were, when they were the ones who did the hit." He told me about one mobster: "When Romeo Martin, a lesser-ranked hood, got it, who the hell do you think were pallbearers? The two guys who whacked him."

He loved to talk about the wives of the made men. Either they were completely submissive or they were tougher than the crime bosses. Teresa was quite gregarious and funny. He loved gossip and regaled me with stories about how tough guys were henpecked and put up with it so the wives wouldn't find out about their girlfriends, who treated them with more respect. He'd chortle and tell me confidentially that of course they knew all about it but saw it as a chance to buy furs and expensive shoes and send their children to parochial school.

Patriarca was overheard on a wiretap giving advice to his son, Raymond Jr.: "Be sure to marry a woman from the old country," he counseled. "She'll always stand by you." By and large, he was correct. The "godmothers" lived very quiet lives. Unlike Carmela of HBO's *The Sopranos*, Mafia wives don't have estates to remodel. While most are native to the United States, the old family values of their Sicilian forebears permeate the way they interact with their husbands and children: "Say nothing, see nothing, hear nothing."

Made guys limited the social activities of their wives. Because they didn't want information to be passed inadvertently, their wives' activities were normally restricted to wakes, weddings, and funerals. The Mafia wife led a life of social isolation. I remembered reading an article in *Time* magazine in May 1977. I saved it. It was by a reporter named Shelley Eichenhorn, who interviewed three middle- to higher-echelon Mafiosi wives. Her story was dead-on.

The women lived suspended in contradictions; tree-lined Grosse Pointe streets and prison cells, family portraits and machine guns.[1] Like the women I met who had just learned what their husbands actually did for a living, the interviewees bristled at the stereotypes of themselves and their families and never believed the headlines. Feeling put-upon by a world that seemed scornful of them, they kept low profiles and kept their thoughts to themselves. Most of the time they were deeply religious Catholics, with statues of saints and sometimes even a chapel in their homes. It was a sad fact that I could almost tell how high-ranking a Mafia guy was by the size of his chapel. The bigger it was, the higher up he was.

One of the women interviewed by Eichenhorn had a plaque proclaiming her "Madonna of the Kitchen." These women

1. *Time*, May 16, 1977, p. 42.

eschewed housekeepers because it was a matter of pride to clean their own house. Certainly, the men were happy at this prospect, too, since they wouldn't have to worry about snooping maids.

Sunday meals with the whole family were observed. The wives would insist on the dinner even when the husband was in jail; the head chair remained unoccupied in honor of the head of the family.

These women suffered slights from the non-Mafia neighborhood women, although the neighbors were pretty discreet so they wouldn't attract retaliation. Children were booted out of some pricey clubs after their fathers went to jail. This turn of events was met with aplomb. The women stood by their children, asserting that the son or daughter was too good for the exclusionists, just as their husband was better than the others.

It was verboten to have the wives witness any violence. They ignored rumors about their husbands' trysts with *comares*. The women seemed to carve out their own quiet lives, since their husbands were often missing because of jail, mistresses, or business activities. No details of the workday were ever discussed at the dinner table.

The wives were keenly aware of the good their spouses did for their neighborhoods. The dons, in particular, had the support of neighbors because they took care of the widows and children and kept peace in the neighborhood. Most of the time the dons earned greater respect than the parish priest or police. In turn, the wives frequently contributed to charities and certainly to the fund-raising drives initiated by their parish. In the poorer neighborhoods, which a lot of Mafia guys were reluctant to leave, the wives were held in high respect.

Sons were encouraged to go to college, as were the daughters. The young ladies, however, were encouraged to marry early in order to extend the influence of a given family. A career for the daughter was frowned upon, except as a lawyer who could help out the family when in need of representation.

When reality intruded upon the idyllic life, it was a very difficult adjustment for a wife who thought of her husband as beleaguered by falsehoods. Wives really took it hard when they had to go into witness protection and be isolated from their extended family. They hated the inability of their children to enjoy aunts and uncles and traditional family gatherings. Despite the hardship, divorce was usually out of the question.

When a son took his place in the mob, the same level of denial inured to his initiation. The son's activities were exempt from maternal inquiry once the son joined the Family. In fact, the daughters were also mum on their brothers' activities or whereabouts.

I must say that I admired most of the wives I met in witness protection. They were Tammy Wynette kind of women who stood by their men and tried to be as supportive as possible of their children. Complaints from them about their treatment were a rarity. Any inconvenience they brought up would be for the children and seldomly for themselves. They lessened the tensions in the relocation by adjusting to the situation. In any other context they'd be viewed as model wives. Many of them were deeply religious.

In some ways these women reminded me of my mother, who faced adversity with equanimity and prayer. She earned a living as a seamstress. My father was a stand-up guy in her father's construction business. My mother's father had kept many a person working during the Depression. The concern for the "extended family"—that is, the community—motivated him as well as my grandfather on my father's side, who did so many nice things for folks that he was affectionately called the Mayor of Cumberland. Ironically, they were the Irish personification of the "family values" that the mob tried to instill in its members.

Vinnie's wife, in particular, was just such a "silent" wife whose entire focus was her home and her three children, David, Cindy, and Wayne. Vinnie told me one day, "So, I said to her, 'I'll take care of makin' the money. You keep your attention on the kids and the house. She neva gave me any static.'"

Occasionally Vinnie would get talking about his life in the mob, usually a bit cocky.

"Take me, a guy who never made it out of the eighth grade. I've beat businessmen, bankers, millionaires, guys with all kinds of education."

He had a respect for religion, although he only went to weddings and funerals. "All the old guys have chapels in their homes. Me, I like religion because my job is tough, and religion keeps me focused." He would pray for success before each of his jobs. Patriotism was high on his list. "Most mob guys I know vote. We vote whatever is the best way to make money with a guy, but we care about the country, too."

One other topic Vinnie Teresa loved to talk about was how certain wise guys got their nicknames. At first I thought this was a bit strange, since he hated being called Fat Vinnie. He'd divert attention from his girth by referencing mob guys who "are really fat, like that Fat Tony Salerno," who was a numbers king in Harlem. Apparently, heavy mobsters like Big Al Polizzi, Angelo "Big Ange" Lonardo, James "Big Jim" Colosimo, Big Joey Massino, Big Paulie Castellano, and others outweighed (pardon the pun) the number of thin guys like Skinny Dom Pizzonia and Skinny Joey Merlino.

I eventually came to believe that Vinnie was regaling me with these stories so I'd think he was truly an insider who knew these fellas well enough to know how they got their names. Many monikers were based on other physical characteristics, like Michael "Mikey Scars" DiLeonardo, who was mauled as a kid by a dog, or George "Muscles" Futterman or Patty "Muscles" Romanello. Sometimes it was the way they dressed or looked, like John "the Dapper Don" Gotti, "Good-looking" Sal Vitale, Joe "Adonis" Doto, or Johnny "Handsome" Roselli.

Since he knew that I had guarded Joe Barboza, Vinnie picked him as the first guy to discuss. It was already quite obvious to me why he was called the Animal, but Vinnie had a whole rap against Barboza, whom he despised. He thought that Barboza killed indiscriminately (true), but then again, *Vinnie* Teresa wasn't *Mother* Teresa. He'd ask me, "Do ya agree?" after he'd dissed Barboza. I'd just let him talk since I thought it would be unprofessional of me to become involved in a discussion about a witness I had guarded previously. Sometimes, Vinnie would slip and refer to Barboza as "the Nigger." He'd quickly follow up and say that wasn't Vinnie's name for Barboza, but that the nickname was out on the streets. "He's sorta dark, as ya know," Vinnie would explain. "He's a Portugee." Actually, I never thought of Barboza as dark-skinned. As a stab at irony, Teresa would say that Barboza hated "Negroes" and had killed at least two guys solely because of their race.

Vinnie could make me laugh as he dished the dirt on other mobsters. Antonio "Joe Batters" Accardo rose through the ranks of the Chicago mob to become boss following the ruthless tactics of his notorious predecessors, Al Capone and Frank Nitti. Accardo retained considerable power after his retirement in 1957 until his death in 1992. With some reverence, Teresa would announce that Accardo got his nickname from the "star" himself, Al Capone. According to Teresa, Capone had arranged a dinner with two turncoats. Accardo walked in with a baseball bat and demolished the skulls of the traitors. As blood splashed on Capone, he announced, "This kid's a real Joe Batters!" How Teresa knew this story was a mystery to me, since it had happened during the Depression, and I never heard that Teresa was linked to any firsthand knowledge. Even today I don't know if it was true, but I just accepted the explanation as Vinnie's attempt to prove his bona fides as a player. "He preferred that name," Teresa said matter of factly when a Chicago newspaper dubbed Accardo "The Big Tuna" after he caught a giant tuna. Accardo at first liked the recognition but then began to think it was a sissified name. Calling him "The Big Tuna" in later life was at your own peril, Vinnie warned.

John "Jackie the Lackey" Cerone was a Chicago hood. He got this name by being the "gofer" and later the chauffeur for Joe Batters. In reality, Cerone was anything but a lackey; or at least, he grew out of the role. He graduated to being an enforcer and later became the boss of "the Outfit," as the Chicago mob was called. After about twenty stints in the hoosegow for a variety of crimes, Cerone was ultimately released from prison in 1996 and died within a week of natural causes at the age of eighty-two.

According to the Teresa lexicon, newspapers would frequently be responsible for a nickname. Anthony "Ant" Spilotro was one such case. Ant was a Chicago mob enforcer who oversaw the family's gambling empire in Las Vegas—well, in a manner of speaking. Ant routinely skimmed profits from the casinos' take. An FBI agent referred to him as "that little pissant" to a reporter in a show of disgust. The editor wouldn't allow this expression to be used in print, so it was shortened to just "Ant." His brothers John, Michael, Victor, and Vincent joined him in a life of crime, leading Teresa to refer to them as "the Ant farm." Ant Spilotro was a particularly vicious killer who would torture his victims and beat them to a pulp. He was responsible for probably more than twenty murders.

Vinnie Teresa would sometimes make a game of dropping names into our conversations, testing me to see if I knew about whom he was talking. "Joey Doves was a birdbrain!" he'd say. When I drew a blank, he'd upbraid me, "Do I hafta teach you everything?" He'd then instruct me that he was referring to Joseph Aiuppa, a Chicago street-crew boss who got pinched transporting doves across state lines. Later, I would find this ironic, since Teresa would engage in a similar importing caper that ultimately brought him down.

"Who's the Artichoke King?" Vinnie asked me. I didn't have a clue. It was Ciro "the Artichoke King" Terranova, a New York City gangster who earned his name because he'd buy crates of artichokes from California and then sell them at a 50 percent profit in New York City. "I've still never heard of the guy," I told Teresa after the explanation. Teresa then laughed and fessed up that the guy had died thirty years earlier. "Not a fair question, Vinnie. You didn't know the guy either." "True, I was just testin' ya!" That ended the hypotheticals, I think, of guys Vinnie didn't know but continued to refer to by their nicknames.

Just so I'd know that Teresa was "in" with young and old mob guys in each of the families throughout the United States, he'd punctuate his conversations with references to guys who were on their last legs. He heaped opprobrium on "Mad Sam" DeStefano, a Chicago mob killer who would eventually die in 1973 at the age of sixty-three. Teresa was disgusted that Mad Sam was a gratuitous torturer of his prey, but Vinnie reserved his real anger for the fact that Mad Sam had killed his own younger brother. "You don't do in your own flesh and blood," he'd sneer. "The whole DeStefano clan is nuts." In any event, DeStefano couldn't have been too deranged, since he made a pile of money fixing cases.

His fees ranged from about $1,000 to fix robbery cases to $20,000 for murder. Corrupt cops would escort defendants to DeStefano's house, get paid, and the suspect would be placed on a "payment plan" of 25 percent interest per week if he didn't have the money up front. If the debtor missed a payment, he'd be invited to the soundproof torture chamber in DeStefano's basement, where he'd dig out some of their flesh as a reminder to pay on time. Usually, the top echelon of the mob would ignore somebody this bad because they'd be heat-seeking missiles for law enforcement, but Mad Sam earned them a lot of money. Their distancing of him, however, was evident by the fact that he wasn't inducted as a made man.

Eventually, DeStefano went on trial for the murder of a rival loan shark, Leo Foreman, whom he had tortured to death. His codefendants were his brother, Mario, and Ant Spilotro. DeStefano started to act strange in public at that time to show he was "insane." He insisted on representing himself, dressed in pajamas, muttered incoherently, and otherwise acted unglued. This behavior would be mimicked by others through the decades to get off the hook. In the murder trial, however, DeStefano's codefendants were getting worried that his antics would result in their convictions. On a Saturday when court was not in session, his codefendants met with him. Allegedly, Spilotro gunned him to death. The mob's Marquis de Sade was dispatched. Spilotro was acquitted of the Foreman murder, while Mario DeStefano, Sam's brother, was found guilty of complicity in the murder.

While I wasn't with Vinnie Teresa when DeStefano was sent to the netherworld, I imagined Vinnie was cheering when he heard the news. As to prove that what goes around comes around, Spilotro's body was found in a cornfield some five miles away from a farm owned by Joey Doves Auippa, who was suspected but never convicted of this murder.

One guy who mimicked DeStefano's "insane" act was a guy Vinnie Teresa liked, by the name of Vincent "The Chin" Gigante. "He's gotta brother, a priest. Can ya explain that?" Vinnie would say with a shrug. He was referring to the fact that the

Chin and three of his brothers belonged to New York's Genovese mob family, while their brother Louis had joined the Diocese of New York. Gigante used to explain his nickname, "the Chin," as a derivation of his Italian mother's pronunciation of "Vincenzo," his given name. Teresa scoffed at the explanation. "I know for a fact," he'd argue, "that the guy was a wipeout as a professional boxer. You'd tap him on his chin, and *bam*, lights out!" Vinnie's assessment was exaggerated. The Chin actually won almost all of his fights and lost four. Perhaps it was his knockout in the first round in a Madison Square Garden fight with Pete Petrello that blurred his other boxing successes.

"He's quite an actor," Vinnie would explain, but with a tone of admiration. Gigante began his mental illness defense in 1969 to dodge multiple prosecutions. I would read that the top echelon New York psychiatrists would all back up his mental disorder defenses, but Vinnie wouldn't hear of it. "He's gonna pretend that he's punch-drunk from all those hits in the ring." Sure enough, knowing that he was always under surveillance, Gigante would pick up cigarette butts off the street and try to smoke them. He'd walk around in a bathrobe, have loud arguments with himself, or drop his pants to urinate. Vinnie would get a kick out of the pants routine: "He's peeing on the feds!" he'd laugh.

This drama went on from 1969 to 1997, when Gigante finally got tagged because Mafia informants brought an end to his play. The jury rang down the curtain on his performance, which had run longer than most Broadway plays. Subsequently, Gigante would acknowledge what Teresa knew all along: his psychosis was a big act.

Vinnie sometimes showed respect by *not* referring to somebody by their nickname. Take Joseph "Joe Bananas" Bonanno, who headed his own crime family. Joe despised his nickname because it implied he was crazy. "He ain't a nutcracker," Vinnie would pronounce. Time seems to have proved Vinnie right, because Bonanno was never convicted of a serious crime and he managed to dodge a lot of attempts to usurp his standing.

While we were passing time before trial with such anecdotes, as well as Teresa's giving me a primer on underground slang (which I already knew, but I humored him like a dutiful student), it was now time for serious business.

Teresa's Boston trial involved a stolen securities case. The defendants were David Iacovetti (a Gambino family soldier), William Dentarmaro and Anthony DeRosa (both members of the Chicago mob and co-crooks with Teresa), and Phil Waggenheim (a strong-arm guy for Ilario Zannino, the number two man in the Boston mob). Vinnie buried them.

Then I took him to Baltimore to testify against mobster Larry Baione regarding the transportation of stolen securities for which Teresa himself had been convicted in 1969. Teresa was facing at least twenty years, so he decided to shave that time by turning in a guy higher up on the totem pole. For him, it was like returning to the scene of the crime.

I arranged for a three-car convoy to drive Teresa about twenty miles from the outskirts to the courthouse in Baltimore. I watched as the marshals checked the cars to make sure they were tamperproof. For example, we'd put a matchstick between the hood and the latch and check to see if it was disturbed. There were other simple tricks of the trade which I won't mention here, since sometimes they are still used. The cars weren't standard government issue; one vehicle would be a station wagon, another a red sedan, another a Jeep.

As we packed Teresa into his vehicle, we followed the protocol of that time. The driver would enter first, the witness entered next and sat in the left rear seat, the deputy would sit next to him, and the supervisor (usually me) would sit in the front right. I got a guy who looked like Vinnie to sit in the backseat of the second car, since the assassins often incorrectly concluded that the pigeon would be in the middle car. Most of the time the decoy was either a law enforcement agent still on duty or a retired cop who was looking for some extra bucks to supplement his pension. Being exposed to a potential assassination didn't bother any of them—it was par for the course. Occasionally, some guys were hired as freelancers. Various law enforcement departments had go-to guys who'd be remunerated for decoy work, such as standing in a lineup. The pay was increased with the risk but was still small potatoes, given the danger. Vinnie's stand-in was a dispatcher whose weight prevented him from becoming a full-fledged cop. Vinnie was in the last car with me.

During the drive, everybody checked the overpasses. We were especially wary of vehicles parked on overpasses, since that provided a favorite sight line from which to kill someone. We maintained our speed just above average and stayed in the flow of traffic. As usual, we rode in the passing lane. It was verboten to ride in the center lane, since it gave two opportunities to get jammed. While we were vigilant throughout the trip, Joe Barboza had taught us that the second-favorite place to target shoot witnesses was at the end of an exit ramp, since we'd have to slow down and turn. With Teresa presenting such a big target, we carefully scanned traffic for overtaking vehicles. The conversation was pretty much nonstop on these trips as the marshals verbally shared their observations.

As we approached our destination, we pulled into Army barracks. I had arranged for a mail truck that I would drive to transport Vinnie on the final leg of the trip to the courthouse. We exchanged vehicles, leaving Vinnie's look-alike in one of the cars. Vinnie was due in court at 10 A.M. I sent the first team of cars in with an escort and screaming sirens. Meanwhile, at ten minutes to 10 A.M., I rode quietly into the underground parking for the courthouse with only one lead car. There was one hitch.

The parking facility had an automatic arm—the lead car made it and the damn thing came down blocking my path. I hadn't realized that it would only allow one vehicle at a time. I slammed on the brakes, and all 350 pounds of Vinnie went tumbling down in the back of the truck. I was afraid I might have knocked him unconscious, since I didn't hear a peep after I got through. When I arrived at my security spot, I rolled up the back of the truck. A vision popped into my head of a headline: "Marshal Does Wise Guy's Job: Kills Star Witness."

"Vinnie, Vinnie," I whispered as I viewed his still-prone body, "Are you all right?" No answer. I started to climb up, beginning to think the worse, when he hissed, "Fuck you." He had been feigning just to get a rise out of me. It worked.

All marshals had Model 10 shotguns for this assignment. Our arms were in direct proportion to the threat, and this was a high alert. The intelligence was that Teresa would be taken out. The mob had to stop the defections. What made the situation even more dangerous for the witness was that the mob lawyers had to be told who would be taking the stand.

At one point during the trial, defendant Baione jumped from his seat and shouted, "You're a lying pig!" which shook up Teresa on the stand. Baione's hoods packed the courtroom and stared Vinnie down. One of the guys in the benches was a hit man from Florida who Vinnie thought had been brought in to kill him.

After his testimony we exited through the same tunnel in the mail truck. This time Vinnie lay on the floor until we got out of the range of the courthouse. Baione was acquitted notwithstanding Teresa's testimony. Teresa was undaunted. "There are stupid juries all the time. That's why we get away with our stuff."

As I mentioned earlier, Teresa was at the La Tuna federal penitentiary near El Paso, Texas, when I began my odyssey with him. Vinnie's family was also relocated to El Paso. That's where he met Joe Valachi, the first made guy to testify against the mob. Teresa would speak very fondly of Valachi. Blanche, Vinnie's wife, would bring pizza, pasta, and other Italian food twice a week for both of them. It was like a mini version of Mafia Row in Lewisberg. Teresa even had a tear in his eye as he recounted Valachi's death while in prison.

Blanche and her family usually stayed put while Vinnie was shuffling from one place to another to testify. My job was to get the kids enrolled in school under their new names. Whenever I had to do this, I would introduce myself as a law enforcement person to the principal (after doing a background check on him) and without explanation would inform him of these kids who would be attending the school and advise him not to send for other school records. Uniformly, these principals would support the effort.

I felt terrible for the children. They had no extended family and couldn't contact past friends or schoolmates. Letters couldn't be written. Contact with outsiders would jeopardize those outsiders, who might be tortured for information. Teresa's kids were particularly homesick for their friends. It was because of the kids that I came up with the idea for mail to be sent to friends and classmates after it was "washed" through two remote postal locations.

Make no mistake about it: the mob was very smart. They'd first check for the location of a witness through insurance. Everybody needs insurance for a house and car. And ex-mobsters had more use for life and boat insurance than your average civilian. To make matters worse, hundreds of insurance companies were owned by the mob. Before this program, many an informant had been rubbed out by a scam: the insurance company would call targets, saying they needed to come in either because they owed a premium or because they had a refund coming.

The mob also had insiders paid off at motor vehicle registries. That's why new identities were necessary, and either I or another marshal (as the program got bigger) would process the day-to-day paperwork.

As part of his deal with the government, Vinnie agreed to testify before the McClellan Commission, which was a congressional committee examining organized crime and the Witness Protection Program. This appearance by Teresa earned him parole.

In some ways Teresa was the star of the show. A favorite line of his was when he was asked about a loan-shark company he ran called Piranha, Inc.

"Why did you call it that name?" a senator asked.

"Because if youse was late paying me, I stuck your hand in a tank of piranhas I kept in my office," Vinnie deadpanned.

The trial earned Teresa a high profile because the committee meetings were televised. He became famous, which increased our problems in protecting him. He was shuttling between trials and grand juries. When his kids were out of school, he and his family were literally "on the road" and staying in hotel rooms. These five rather large people were eating, drinking, and conversing, day in and day out, in cramped quarters. Stress was taking its toll on the kids, and they were putting on a lot of weight. I had a level of respect for their equanimity in the circumstances. Teresa was a patient father with his children, and his wife was the very model of a dutiful spouse. I never heard a complaint or a cross word out of her mouth.

The biggest stress was safety. The mob would have loved to have silenced Teresa by kidnapping a member of his family. The marshals watched his kids like hawks.

One time two guys were casing the street during one of Teresa's court appearances in Boston. One of them had a leg cast on. The FBI asked Vinnie if he knew who these men were. Teresa knew immediately that the man with the cast was a small-time hood named Tommy Rossi. Rossi always used the broken-leg routine to case banks before he robbed them.

When it appeared that Vinnie was going to exit our program once he had finished testifying, we began transition planning. Vinnie was all nerved up. He'd been on a government subsidy of $1,800 per month far beyond the usual period because he wasn't a good candidate for a job. He lucked out when a reporter approached him and he landed a book deal worth $175,000, good money in the early seventies. Vinnie talked and the reporter wrote. Vinnie was supposed to appear on the *Merv Griffin Show* to pump sales. There was a raging debate about whether he should fulfill his contract with the publisher and do the publicity. I decided we could do that trek, particularly after Vinnie was begging me to put him in the TV spotlight again. He missed the notoriety engendered from his McClellan Commission appearance. Off we went to California. The show aired, and on the way back we were flying on Continental Airlines. All of a sudden the stewardess took a look at Vinnie and loudly proclaimed to the passengers that there was a celebrity on board.

"Let me see," she said. "I have your name on the tip of my tongue. I know who you are. I just saw you on television."

The passengers were all transfixed.

"Miss," I responded, "allow me to introduce you to Minnesota Fats." Minnesota Fats was a popular pool player at the time who weighed about the same as Vinnie. While he never won a major tournament, he was so flashy that people thought he was more successful than he was.

"I knew it! I knew it!" she responded. "My boyfriend loves pool, and you're his hero." She left momentarily and returned with a pad of paper. "Will you sign an autograph for him?"

"Sure," Vinnie said in his most charming voice, scribbling "Minnesota Fats" on the paper. I wanted to die laughing.

Later, on the way back to his quarters, Vinnie gave me more history on mobsters' nicknames. In case there was a wiretap, they used only nicknames. All were codes. Big boss Raymond Patriarca was always referred to as George on the phone. Other nicknames, like Vinnie's own, Fat Vinnie, were descriptive. Joe "Beans" Palladino got the name because he ate kidney beans every day. Lou "the Gimp" Greco limped from a war injury and so on. I was getting a little sick of this constant chatter, but when the time came to bid the Teresa family good-bye, it was strange—I was going to miss him. Despite being suspicious of me initially, he actually began to like me. He was a natural comic. Unlike the mercurial Barboza, Teresa was a laugh a minute. I suspected that my other protectees would be dull by comparison. Little did I know I'd be back in Vinnie Teresa's life in just a few months.

With the success of Vinnie Teresa's testimony, the program continued to grow by leaps and bounds. One afternoon I found myself running up and down a staircase in a New York hotel between the fifth floor—a mobster's wife, mother, and four children, all worried about their new life now that another gunman was going to testify against the mob—and the third floor—a different gangster's girlfriend crying inconsolably because she had been forced to disappear due to her married lover's decision to testify against the mob. As I was juggling their concerns, my phone rang.

"We got a hot one," my new boss, Reis Kash, head of WITSEC (Witness Security Program) said. "Leave right now and get this woman to safety."

Like always, it was raining. It was a Friday afternoon and the streets were jammed with vehicles as I tried to get to the Bronx. I was just imagining how frightened this woman must be while she was waiting for me. Kash had told me that she had inadvertently been privy to a conversation at a car lot owned by her boss about the great job he had done murdering someone. As a good citizen she had informed the FBI, and now her boss was trying to silence her permanently.

I finally got there and parked in an alley. I viewed the scene outside and saw nothing. I had no backup, but time was of the essence, so I proceeded.

"Who's there?" a shaky voice inquired as I rapped on the door.

"John Partington, U.S. deputy marshal."

"How can I be sure?"

I held up my ID and badge to the peephole. She opened the door a crack, and I saw a child of about ten years old clutching her dress. The child was clearly frightened.

"Ready to go?" I asked.

"We gotta take my daughter's rabbit." She nodded to a wire cage. I wasn't thrilled about tying up a free hand in case of a struggle, but I knew that the child had been scared enough and the rabbit would calm her, so I scooped it up. Fortunately, I had beaten the clock. We got into my car.

En route to the motel where I was going to stash them, the mother had a thousand questions—all relevant, but I didn't know the answers. I just told her not to worry, that things would be taken care of, and that right now I would keep them safe.

During the three-hour drive to the motel, they both fell asleep. Upon arrival, I checked them into the motel and gave her $100 in cash for groceries along with emergency numbers to call, including mine. The dead bolt clicked behind me. I stationed myself across the street at a tavern and ordered a whiskey, which I nursed for forty-five minutes. Every five minutes I looked over at the motel to make sure nobody had followed us. On the way there I had constantly checked the rearview mirrors and done driving maneuvers which should have outed anybody following us. It was safe to go. I left for Providence, a four-hour drive.

I hadn't been home for three weeks and I was desperate to see my family. I had told Helen I would be home for the entire weekend, but now it was the wee hours of Saturday morning. Guilt also hung over me like a cloud since my son, Scott, had recently accused me of caring more for my gangster charges than for him. I finally arrived shortly before daybreak. No sooner had I gotten into the house, showered, and crawled into bed then the phone rang.

"Better get out here fast," the motel clerk told me. "The woman you checked in just woke me up. There's blood everywhere."

It was a four-hour return trip. She had a gash the size of a pen on her forehead. She had slipped taking a shower and banged her head on the towel rod. Off we went to an emergency room, where I gave a false name for her and paid cash for her treatment. On the way back to the hotel she admonished me: "What took you so long? Suppose there had been a real emergency?"

I sat in silence. She had a point. The program was stretched too thin, the demands were overwhelming the manpower. I had proposed forging partnerships with selected police officers in various towns, but my bosses had vetoed the proposal. There was a deep reluctance to involve other law enforcement personnel. Some of the objections were valid, such as potential crooked cops on the mob's pad, but could have been screened out. I felt the main objection was agency hubris, which persists in law enforcement today. Sometimes I was getting just an hour's sleep, running on pure adrenaline.

While I continued the shuffle of witnesses, I learned that Vinnie Teresa was going to reenter protection. The Feds had relocated him to Fishkill, New York, where the government had given him a stake to open up a fish market. Occasionally, he'd call me and tell me to await a shipment of lobsters.

According to Gerald Shur, a prosecutor who worked with Teresa and who cowrote the book *WITSEC: Inside the Federal Witness Protection Program*, other fish dealers were complaining that someone was breaking their store windows and doing nasty tricks to slow down their business. Teresa had to be relocated. Before being whisked out of town, Teresa sold the refrigeration units in his store, which were rented by the government. Lucky for him, his peccadilloes were overlooked because of the big fish he had reeled in for the FBI.

His next venture with the aid of Uncle Sam was to buy a hotel in El Paso, Texas. Vinnie called me up to share how successful the opening was. "Every politician was here," he said, "including the governor, a U.S. senator, and a congressman." He didn't last long as a hotelier. One night he consumed too much of his own booze and climbed up on the bar, which was no mean accomplishment.[2] He yelled for the crowd to be quiet.

"Do you know who I am?" he roared.

"John Cantino!" the crowd shouted back. Cantino was Teresa's new name. I thought it was funny, since "cantino" meant singer in Italian, and he had done plenty of singing against his cohorts.

"Noooo! I'm Vinnie Teresa, the famous mob guy!" The patrons laughed in confusion. That was his last day.

Gerald Shur also tells the story that as they were about to relocate him, Vinnie drove his car filled with liquor from his erstwhile bar up the ramp into a truck. He sold both his car and the booze, even though the liquor was bought on credit.

---

2. Pete Earley and Gerald Shur, *WITSEC: Inside the Federal Witness Protection Program* (New York: Bantam, 2002), 111.

Teresa couldn't stay out of the spotlight. There's an attraction to being at the center of attention that Joe Barboza had also missed.

Soon Vinnie Teresa was announcing that he could bring down the legendary mobster Meyer Lansky, the Cosa Nostra's financial advisor and casino operator. He claimed that he had personally taken bags of unreported cash to Lansky in Miami. He convinced the prosecutors and a grand jury to indict Lansky. At the time of the grand jury testimony, Lansky was in Israel. I'm convinced that Teresa thought he'd never come back. He was wrong: Lansky returned, was promptly arrested, and the trial was on.

A marshal detail stowed Teresa in the Everglades as the launching pad for bringing him to a court in Miami to testify. I was dispatched to Florida for the upcoming trial to make sure he lived to appear on the stand.

As soon as I got to the holding area, I knew it was all wrong. It was sixty miles out of Miami. Vinnie didn't look good to me. He was subdued, which was very odd, given his bombastic nature. He looked as though a vampire had drained his blood. I ordered the marshals to move him closer to Miami. With some skepticism and resentment, the deputies complied. En route to the new location, Vinnie started to have terrible chest pains. Off to a hospital we went. He had suffered a heart attack. The doctor said he would have been a goner if he hadn't received immediate treatment, and the men looked at me with new respect.

Ironically, Meyer Lansky himself was getting postponements on the basis of having a bad heart. It's hard to tell whether this was true. Raymond Patriarca and other mobsters always came up with "heart trouble" to escape a trial. Later, this excuse was replaced by Alzheimer's. In any event, after a series of postponements, the trial was going to start for real.

Meyer Lansky was on trial for income tax evasion because of

the bagfuls of money Vinnie had allegedly brought him from gambling junkets.

Vinnie didn't look like his usual self at this point. To avoid identification, he had lost weight and now sported a professorial goatee. He entered the courthouse dressed in a suit and tie and carrying a briefcase. He looked like a lawyer accompanying another legal eagle, who was actually a marshal.

Vinnie was okay on direct examination. When the prosecution finished the questioning after a couple of hours, the defense attorney, David Rosen, pounced. It was clear that this was an issue of credibility. The jury had not been informed about Lansky's past. Rosen did a great job of establishing that Vinnie was an accomplished liar. The pièce de résistance was when Vinnie couldn't describe the house where he had allegedly dropped off the dough, let alone remember Lansky's address. Bad went to worse when it was learned that Lansky was in Boston getting a hernia repair on the day Teresa allegedly gave him the cash. I knew the inevitable verdict: not guilty on the main count. To this day, I don't know whether Vinnie was deliberately lying initially, since it seemed at trial that he didn't want to testify against Lansky. I had my suspicions that he missed the limelight and wanted to be back on Uncle Sam's payroll, but my job was to keep him alive, not to stop his gravy train. The higher up the food chain you implicated someone, like Lansky, the more perks you were given.

Many times Vinnie railed on and on about Frank Sinatra. First he said Sinatra was involved in the mob. Then he'd say that Sinatra was a friend of mobsters, which was probably true. Then it was that Sinatra owed his career to the mob. Later Teresa acknowledged that Sinatra had talent and could have made it on his own but added that he didn't take to Sinatra's arrogance. I felt Teresa was practicing a story to see if it would fly and get him more government benefits.

Vinnie soon left the marshals' protection again after the Lansky trial and went into another business with the help of the FBI. That business got him in further trouble. While he'd no longer be a songbird for the government, he would become a jailbird.

First, Vinnie was sentenced to a ten-year jail term on mail fraud and cocaine charges while he ran a pet store, compliments of the government's down payment. Back in those days, there were no forfeiture provisions as in today's racketeering statute. He stayed a short time in prison while his son carried on the business. Shortly after his parole, Vinnie and his son, David, were arrested and charged for smuggling endangered birds and reptiles into the United States. No joke. Technically, Teresa was still in the relocation program when his appetite for trafficking parrots, blue-eyed tritons, great sulfur-crested cockatoos, goffins, and extremely rare reptiles known as Komodo dragons was wheted. The charges stemmed from 1978 to 1980, when he and his son operated an exotic bird business in Seattle.

When I heard about the charges, I thought how ingenious this guy was at making a buck. The birds and the cold-blooded invertebrates summed up his character. He was making tens of thousands of dollars in the smuggling operation. I felt bad that his family was brought into it. His other son, Wayne Cantino, was dropped as a codefendant in the scheme since he was serving a life term at the Washington State Penitentiary for a drug-related murder. Vinnie and David pled guilty under a plea agreement whereby charges were dropped against the twenty-nine-year-old David's wife and Vinnie's daughter Cindy, age thirty-two. This was truly a family affair. David was fined $1,000 and placed on three-years probation. Vinnie got two more years in the slammer.

Eventually, Vinnie Teresa died in obscurity in 1990 at the age of sixty-one. As a man who fingered millions in his life, he died pretty poor. The Marshals Service sent a deputy to pay his funeral bill.

In 2006 I was talking to a police officer who had worked for me while I served my stint as commissioner of public safety in Providence. He was telling me about a bank robber who had just been arrested in the capital city. The guy had passed a note to a bank teller demanding "50s, 30s [*sic*] and 20s." A Mensa member he was not. We reminisced about other Bonnies and Clydes who were harebrained. One guy passed out when he was told that the teller had no cash. He was still on the floor when the police arrived. They had to revive him. Another gent in the neighboring city of Cranston robbed an armored car containing only $3,200 in pennies. He was caught about thirty yards away, out of breath from lugging the loot.

This walk down memory lane prompted me to recall a robber I had protected who was a modern-day John Dillinger. He was involved in the infamous Bonded Vault robbery and after a career of nonstop holdups, he came into the Witness Protection Program because of his willingness to testify against other mob guys involved in this heist of more than $4 million. His name was Robert Dussault, a hood who had been involved in at least a dozen robberies netting large amounts of cash.

The Bonded Vault case was notorious in its day. On August 14, 1975, nine masked men entered a commercial safe-deposit company in broad daylight, robbed its employees at gunpoint, and broke into 146 safe-deposit boxes. Dussault, who told police that he had been a participant, was granted immunity for testifying against six of his cohorts, including reputed organized crime members Gerard T. Ouimette, Ralph Byrnes, and Charles Flynn. All three were convicted, including Ouimette, who had not physically participated in the robbery, while three others were acquitted during the ten-week trial. No reason was given as to why Dussault wasn't forced to testify against all of the participants, although one other, Joseph Danese, was also given immunity to testify against the gang members.

The case went on forever, with appeal after appeal. In all, it stretched from 1975 through 1991, with various grounds urged for the reversal of the convictions. Defendant Ouimette had married an attorney who had been a tenacious public defender, so she pulled out all the stops to set him free from prison.

During the time my marshals were guarding Dussault, we learned valuable lessons. While there was a round-robin of legal arguments to free the convicted defendants, including one based on prosecutorial misconduct for failure to disclose to the defense team some twenty-eight crimes committed by the star witness (he had a repertoire of other crimes besides bank robberies), the ground for appeal that most hit home for me was the one involving the seating of four state troopers in the front row behind the defendants for the jury to see during their trial. If you ever saw the uniform of the Rhode Island State Troopers, you'd know they were impressive. Indeed, several state police officers appeared on the *Late Show with David Letterman* after they won Best Uniform in a national contest. With their high boots, jodhpurs, tailored shirts, and Stetson hats, they were a sight to behold. The defendants' counsel objected to the seating of the troopers in their full regalia on the basis that their presence threw an aura of guilt and the suggestion of violence on the defendants' part. The Rhode Island supreme court rejected the argument and supported the trial judge's ruling denying the motion to remove the troopers.

The defendants next brought a habeas corpus petition in federal court. The federal district court judge bought the suggestibility argument, and the defendants struck gold further at the First Circuit Court of Appeals. This court upheld the reversal of the convictions on the basis that the presence of the troopers, so dressed, was inherently prejudicial and overly suggestive of both guilt and the defendants' penchant for violence. The state appealed, and it wasn't until 1986, long after I ceased being the marshal in charge of the Witness Protection Program, that the U.S. Supreme Court reversed the vacating of the conviction and ruled that the mere presence of troopers was just as likely to have been taken as a sign of a normal official concern for safety and order. The convictions stood. Further legal issues to free the defendants stretched the case out until 1991.

Of course, during my tenure I didn't know how the court would ultimately rule on the presence of the uniforms in the courtroom, but I was aware of the argument raging on this issue from 1976 forward. I decided not to make the same mistake, so I had my guys dress casually in the court, and they would stay only when the protected witness was on the stand. The Bonded Vault trial took place during the steamy summer, so the troopers had looked a bit odd fully decked out. My guys protecting witnesses would wear bulky sports shirts in the courtrooms during summer months, which disguised the guns they were carrying.

I also became aware that in order to blend into the spectator section, I needed more than white males as marshals. I sought and finally got a black marshal and a woman after many months of lobbying my bosses at headquarters. I remember the day they arrived on my doorstep with Joe Thomas, a white marshal around the age of twenty-five. He, along with Melvin H. Graham, my first black marshal, and Patricia Melleney, my first female marshal, reminded me of the actors in a popular TV show at the time, *The Mod Squad*. I promptly dubbed them that amid their laughter at the appellation. I wanted to use them immediately, so I introduced them to the law enforcement elite in Rhode Island for intensive training. They learned from the best, which included Colonel Walter Stone of the Rhode Island State Police, Major Pete Benjamin, Lieutenant Nat Urso, Pawtucket Police standout Ted Dolan, Jack Leydon, a major in the Providence police squad, and two Providence cops who were specialists in organized crime at the time: Vinnie Vespia and Anthony Mancuso. The mod squad was a quick study. Within weeks I was so comfortable that they had learned the ropes that I assigned them to transport and guard Dussault. They did a great job and went on to top promotions in the service.

When I rendezvoused with them and the other marshals guarding Dussault, I would take the time to talk with Dussault about many things regarding his "vacation" with us, including his career as a bank robber. I figured I could get a free education by learning how he thought. Robert Dussault was a bad dude. He had actually escaped from a Massachusetts prison where he still had twenty-one years to serve a sentence for a bank robbery. He was arrested in Las Vegas, where he promptly negotiated a deal of no jail time to rat out his partners in the Bonded Vault caper. I thought it was obvious that another deal had been cut, since the Massachusetts authorities knew Dussault was in Rhode Island custody, yet they filed no paperwork to have him returned to Massachusetts to serve his sentence when his utility was exhausted. Furthermore, no effort was made to add years to his sentence for the escape. He also had another indictment for a robbery of a bank in Worcester, Massachusetts, for which he pled guilty and received a minimum sentence from which he was immediately paroled. These free passes probably explained his arrogance. I figured he was singing the equivalent of an opera against other hoodlums to get these breaks.

Dussault certainly liked to brag about his exploits. With nerves of steel, he usually used weapons in his holdups. "Using a note to pass to a teller is a sissy way to rob a bank," he said. He wanted a gun in the teller's face. "Makes 'em hurry up," he explained. He'd bring his own duffel bags to the bank, since subtlety was not his style. While today's robbers do the so-called "note jobs," back in Dussault's day, only about one third of robberies were done this way. Macho was in. Remember also that the technology for committing bank fraud wasn't that far developed in the seventies. Banks also had much more cash available in the registers during the seventies. Today, the usual take is a few thousand dollars at most.

In some ways Dussault's exploits blanch in comparison to today's Internet thefts. Billions of dollars are looted through identity theft, credit scams, and phishing (tricking consumers into divulging financial information). Because these schemes are global in nature, the electronic bandits are often able to elude capture. I sometimes think back and wonder whether guys like Dussault would be an anachronism in today's robbery world. I suspect that he didn't have the brainpower that Red Kelley, my next charge, had in his heyday, and perhaps he'd have been considered only a meat-and-potatoes hood by current standards. Then again, he was smart enough to figure out that the safe-deposit box owners at Bonded Vault, with bearer bonds, jewelry, cash, and other valuables, might be good patsies since they might have been hiding their wealth from Uncle Sam. He was nonetheless a lesser robber in terms of skills, brains, and moxie than the next guy I had to protect.

9

ARMORED TRUCK HEISTS

'll never forget the first time I met Red Kelley. His ruddy-complexioned face reminded me of a giant leprechaun's. Shocks of gray ran through his thinning red mane. At six foot one, he was two inches taller than me and built like a cement block.

The first thing out of his mouth was "I know you. You're Partington. Good to meet you, John." Next he ran down a list of people he had been ordered to kill while I had been guarding them, including Joe Barboza. "I couldn't get near 'em," he said. "That's when I decided that if I ever needed to, I'd go into Witness Protection because you could protect me." Dubious praise, but I have to admit I was flattered.

"So, let's get to it right now." He brought me over to a window and pointed to a construction crew that was working at the military base where he was being held. He identified several of Patriarca's hoods, such as Bobo Marrapese and Rudy Sciarra, whom he had spotted the previous day when he was taking his exercise in the yard.

"If these goons spot me, I'm history. Get me outta here."

Under cover of night, I moved him to Pease Air Force Base in New Hampshire.

John "Red" Kelley, a freelance hit man for the mob, was a

meticulous planner. Kelley knew that he could never be a made man because he was Irish, but he was still valued for his dispatch of Raymond Patriarca's enemies. He also was a genius when it came to planning heists.

On August 14, 1962, on Route 3 in Plymouth, Massachusetts, a mail truck was en route to Boston. The banks on Cape Cod were transporting their excess cash to the Federal Reserve Bank. Initially, they had paid for state police escorts to accompany the mail trucks, but eventually the banks became penny wise but dollar foolish. Two postal employees manned the truck: one a driver, and the other a guard. Both carried the equivalent of peashooters as sidearms.

Kelley observed everything about the route of the drivers for six months. He was greatly emboldened when the state police detail fell off in July 1962. Finally, after he had examined every possible angle of the heist, the robbery was to go down.

At about 8 P.M., a member of Kelley's team dressed as a Plymouth cop appeared on the road and, pointing to a detour sign, directed the truck to a more deserted road because, as the "police officer" explained, there had been an "accident" that had closed the highway. On the deserted road, a gun moll of one of the robbers played a damsel in distress. The two postal employees left the truck to help the attractive young woman. Several masked gunmen then jumped from two cars parked at the roadside and forced them to open up their truck. Tied with duct tape to one of the stolen cars, the captives watched as two robbers dressed as armored car drivers drove off with the truck. At a preplanned destination in Randolph, Massachusetts, Kelley's crew unloaded the loot. It was at least a $1.5 million payday.

Jerry Angiulo, the mob boss in Boston, had financed the operation. He fronted about $7,000 for the bogus uniforms, the shotguns, and masks. The arrangement was for Angiulo to front the money and hold on to the stolen loot until it was safe to circulate. He had plenty of contacts in financial institutions who could advise him when the money had "cooled." Further, he had many legit operations in which he could bury the money: he owned a hospital in Boston and a bowling alley in Florida and he co-owned a golf course with Raymond Patriarca. This course is still in existence but owned by another party, so I won't name it.

There is some controversy over whether the job was planned by Red Kelley or another hoodlum. In his book *My Life in the Mafia*,[1] Vinnie Teresa gives credit to another guy, Billy Aggie, as the planner. In any event, Billy didn't make it to the party because he was ill the night of the job. Red Kelley executed the heist. He fenced the money to Angiulo, keeping an unheard of 80 percent for himself rather than the more typical 60 percent fee for the robber, 40 percent to the mob boss.

When Aggie got out of the hospital, he demanded his share. Kelley played it that Aggie never had much to do with the heist. Aggie went to Angiulo to settle his claim, and Angiulo called a meeting of the heist team. Red had no intention of sharing any loot with the others; he was going to pay them for their involvement with a bullet.

Two guys involved in the robbery were shot and killed before the meeting. Others who had heard about the holdup participants were likewise dispatched. Robert Rasmussen, a Dedham, Massachusetts, wise guy was shot in the head. He was found dressed only in his underwear, black socks, and a necktie. Another wise guy, Frankie Benjamin, was found dead on Tenean Beach. Red Kelley had lucked out; Frankie had another enemy, Vincent aka Jimmy "the Bear" Flemmi. Both had been in Walpole State Prison together, although Frankie had been paroled first. One night, while Frankie was drinking at

---

1. Vincent Charles Teresa, *My Life in the Mafia* (Garden City, NY: Doubleday, 1973).

a taproom, the Bear entered. Accounts are vague as to what happened next, but the Bear shot Benjamin in the head. Because the Bear had used a cop's gun, he decided to saw off the victim's head so ballistics couldn't trace the gun. There was so much blood on the floor from the decapitation that the gangsters decided to torch the place to get rid of any evidence. Benjamin's body was dumped in the back of a stolen car sans head, which was never recovered. They didn't want a body in the bar because the owners would no doubt try to collect insurance for the "unfortunate" fire. Thereafter Angiulo delivered a message from Raymond Patriarca that the Bear couldn't keep killing because people were starting to look at Flemmi the wrong way, but the Bear didn't follow Patriarca's directive. Benjamin's murder was unsolved for many years, until the Bear got pinched through an informant.

Two more mobsters involved in the heist were also killed. Leo Lowry, another graduate of Walpole, was shot to death and his throat was slit. George Ash was also slain in the South End of Boston. In the end, Aggie collected nothing. There was nobody around to testify as to Aggie's role in the robbery.

Kelley was indicted in 1967 for the Plymouth mail robbery, but the charges were dropped because of insufficient evidence. He was also implicated in the robbery of an armored truck in Fall River, Massachusetts. The holdup yielded $177,000, which was never recovered. This crime was also not prosecuted.

As a stone-faced hit man, Kelley's reputation was that he'd lie with rattlesnakes to get a hit. He was considered the front-runner on orders from Raymond Patriarca to hit Willie Marfeo, a bookmaker who was trying to run independent games on Federal Hill. Patriarca wanted a cut, so he sent Henry Tameleo, his number two guy, to make arrangements for a kickback in exchange for letting Marfeo run his games on the Hill. Marfeo originally said he'd pay but did not cough up his tribute.

Tameleo went to reason with him one more time. "Look, Willie, this is your last warning."

Marfeo slapped Tameleo in the mouth. "Get out of here, old man. Go tell Raymond to go shit in his hat. We're not giving you anything."

"Mister, you are a dead man," said a furious Tameleo. "Go pay your insurance."

Unbeknownst to Patriarca, there was a wiretap planted in his office that picked up Tameleo's recitation of the event when he returned to brief the crime boss. Patriarca was livid. Respect is a big thing. Young guys were expected to defer to their elders: they'd give up a seat, they'd bow and scrape. Marfeo crossed the line; his life was to be snuffed for the breach.

For reasons that are uncertain, Patriarca passed over Kelley and imported an outsider to hit Marfeo. On July 13, 1966, Willie Marfeo scarfed down his last pizza at the Korner Kitchen restaurant on Federal Hill. A stranger came into the restaurant, made everybody lie on the floor, and took Marfeo out to a phone booth, where he plugged him. The phone booth had been used by Marfeo to process his betting business, so the lesson was very clear. The murderer escaped into the crowd and Mafia blindness descended upon the pedestrians; nobody saw anything.

Patriarca's trouble did not abate—Willie Marfeo had a headstrong younger brother named Rudy who was out to exact revenge. Patriarca wanted to stop him, but Rudy was very careful. He never followed the same routine from one day to the next. Red Kelley had two more nicknames: Swiss Watch, because he was so methodical, and Saint John, since he had infinite patience. Kelley was Patriarca's man for the job.

Kelley studied Rudy Marfeo for weeks and was rewarded for his time. The one predictable part of Rudy Marfeo's schedule was that he would visit a certain grocery store after he played golf. Kelley practiced the run from the golf course over and over again at all the times that Marfeo might leave the course. When he had it down pat, he went to New York to get sawed-off shotguns, a carbine, and Halloween masks. He recruited Maurice "Pro" Lerner, John E. Rossi, and Richard Fairbrothers to do the actual hit; Kelley would be the supervisor. Pro Lerner got his nickname because he almost made it to the major leagues in baseball. Pro continued to use his skills; on one Patriarca-ordered hit, he killed a guy who answered the door with a single swing of his baseball bat across the guy's head.

On the day of the rubout, Kelley was with "friends" at the golf course, all decked out like golfers. When Rudy left, Kelley followed and signaled to his cohorts to kill Rudy in the grocery store. Rudy and his golfing pal Anthony Melei were riddled with bullets. It was another Sicilian Vespers.[2]

Everything worked like clockwork for Kelley. It was not until he decided to participate in the robbery of a Brink's truck in 1968 that he got his comeuppance.

When a Boston North End hood named Phil Cresta set his sights on hitting a Brink's truck, Kelley was his man. Cresta knew of the robbers' fates in the Plymouth mail truck incident, so he did not really trust Kelley, but he enlisted Kelley anyway because of Kelley's expertise. Besides, Cresta was sure of his own skills to control Kelley.

Cresta had made the acquaintance of a Brink's guard. It was great having a man on the inside. Hedging his bets, Cresta had Kelley meet with the insider, Andrew DeLeary. Cresta thought that he'd be protecting the rest of his team: if DeLeary punked out, the only person he'd be able to finger was Red Kelley. Cresta knew that the Feds wanted Kelley bad, so Cresta would be able to cut a deal.

---

2. "Sicilian Vespers" is slang for a kill.

Red Kelley clocked an armored truck that had pickups at restaurants, hospitals, and three department stores: Filene's, Jordan Marsh, and Raymond's. Kelley was beside himself with the prospect of a large take right before the Christmas holidays. He got the rest of his colleagues to eschew several plans of picking off other Brink's armored vehicles in favor of this hit.

Painstaking efforts were made to case the route of Brink's truck no. 6280. From mid-October to mid-November, the gang regularly clocked the Saturday route. On Saturdays, because of the size of the loot, the truck had three guards. The guards always ate at the same places. The last stop was Downey & Judges, a bar on Canal Street. Two guards would go into the bar while the third stayed in the back of the truck. Although the truck was locked, the guard inside never bolted any of the doors. Kelley decided to make keys to open the truck, because by happenstance DeLeary was assigned to truck no. 6280.

Here's how the keys were made. Predictably, the guards' routine continued, only this time DeLeary was one of the two guards who got out for a food break. One of the gang was in a phone booth seven yards from the pit stop. As he pretended to be talking to someone, DeLeary passed the keys to him in the blink of an eye. The guy then walked around the corner to Cresta, who was sitting in a car with a key-making machine. It took him all of two minutes to make each key, one for the truck's front door, the other for the back. The originals were deposited into the coin-return slot of the phone in the same phone booth just moments before DeLeary and the other guard emerged from the bar. As prearranged, DeLeary told his partner that he had to make a brief call and pocketed the keys.

Kelley and Cresta weren't done yet. Kelley gave the copied keys to DeLeary to test. After confirming that both keys were a perfect fit, De Leary scratched an "F" on the key for the front door. The stage was now set for a hit on December 14, 1968.

On December 13, Cresta and Kelley arranged for getaway cars (stolen, from unsuspecting owners). Things were running like clockwork. But just as the heist was about to go down, Cresta noticed that one of their getaway cars had been stolen by somebody unknown. The mission was postponed to the following Saturday.

On Saturday, December 21, about three minutes before the heist, two of Cresta's hoods, who stood guarding the replacement getaway cars, a block and a half away from the intended crime scene suddenly heard a voice: "What the hell are you doing here? Somebody let you greaseballs out of your cage for the day or something?"

The voice belonged to a detective who, along with the cop standing beside him, worked for the Boston Police's organized crime unit. With the detectives in the vicinity, the robbery was postponed again. The thieves were lucky that the cops didn't check the vehicles' registrations.

Cresta bemoaned the loss of at least $1.5 million, since the next Saturday's take would be after the Christmas rush.[3] Red Kelley went ballistic after the second cancellation of the job. "This fuckin' job is jinxed!" he roared.

One thing I learned from mob witnesses I protected was that the successful ones followed their superstitions. By the following Saturday, December 28, 1968, Kelley had bowed out of the scheme, pretending to have a bad cold. The score went down. After driving off with the truck, the robbers emptied the loot from the back. Nobody noticed that the key was still in the front door lock. After transferring the money into a series of cars, the group thought they were safe. The money was divvied up. Kelley demanded his share even though he

---

3. Brian P. Wallace and Bill Crowley, *Final Confession: Unsolved Crimes of Phil Cresta* (Northeastern University Press, 2008).

had begged off. Cresta gave Kelley $65,000 for assisting in the planning.

"You'll be able to pay your doctor for the miraculous cure he gave you for your cold," one of the team sniped at Kelley.

Things worked out well for about three months. Then Red Kelley called Phil Cresta. Kelley had been calling DeLeary every few days to make sure he wasn't spending any of the money but hadn't reached him. Cresta acknowledged that he hadn't spoken to Deleary for about ten days. Then the bad news came. DeLeary was supposed to be sitting on the dough but instead was sitting on a beach chair in the Bahamas with his extended family, compliments of the Brink's truck proceeds.

Needless to say, the Feds put two and two together, and De-Leary was eventually carted off to the hoosegow. DeLeary's comrades tried to rub him out but never got a clear hit. DeLeary fingered them all once he was taken into custody. In turn, Kelley got religion and agreed to testify against his cohorts in order to cut his own break.

While the cops were rounding up the gang, Phil Cresta managed to escape the dragnet. At the trial, Kelley and De-Leary buried their cohorts: while they each got three to five years, the others were hit with twenty-five to forty years in prison. Cresta was still on the lam. During his exile, he met several times with James Whitey Bulger. Bulger paid rapt attention to the lessons on hiding that Phil Cresta shared with him. Many years later, Whitey Bulger would implement the advice very well. Cresta was finally caught in 1974 and made to answer for this crime and others. Due in large part to Kelley's testimony, Cresta was found guilty for the Brink's robbery and sentenced to twenty-five to forty years. He died of heart trouble while in prison.

Red Kelley, on the other hand, was not one to spend any time in jail. Immediately after his testimony against the other

Brink's thieves, he dispatched F. Lee Bailey, a noted Boston lawyer, to speak with the Feds about a deal. Kelley promised to testify against a slew of organized-crime wise guys, including "the Man," Raymond Patriarca. Based on this offer, Kelley was placed in protective custody on June 4, 1969, and was held at Otis Air Force Base in Falmouth, Massachusetts, where our relationship began.

Red Kelley told me outlandish stories that sounded convincing. He swore up and down that he was part of a $4 million hit team recruited by mob boss Sam Giancana with the permission of Patriarca to assassinate Fidel Castro. The team was to consist of Kelley and Pro Lerner. He informed me that originally Giancana and Patriarca declined any CIA money because they thought it was their patriotic duty to assassinate the Cuban leader. Effort after effort was mounted, using poison, lethal pills, and so on. Then, frustrated by the mob's rising costs, they agreed to take the money and do it the old-fashioned way by plugging Castro. The White House gave the okay, Kelley asserted, dropping the name of Robert Matheu, a former FBI agent, as his point man. The caper didn't go down because word had gotten around that the Kennedys were cheerleading Castro's demise, which was forbidden under international law. Years later, when classified documents were released, I would read that Matheu was involved in trying to take out Castro. To this day though, I don't know what to believe of Kelley's story. The mob had a rumor mill to match that of law enforcement, so Kelley could have been privy to these facts from his exposure to the whispers.

Red Kelley was the most secretive man I ever met. I still don't know whether he had any children. The only way I even learned that he had a wife was when he informed me in 1971 that she was sick in a Connecticut hospital and he wanted to visit her. I accommodated his request. He insisted that we not go into the hospital room, because that would send up red flags, so I had his wife moved to a room where there was a glass partition so we could watch him at all times.

"How is she doing?" I asked after the three-hour visit, but Kelley was tight-lipped. In case anybody had gotten a bead on this trip, I arranged to move Kelley to a location in Seekonk, Massachusetts. Several more times we went to the hospital, and each time I'd change the return address.

Anyone who had crossed paths with Red Kelley would say Kelley was tough, so they might have been surprised to hear two things: first, he loved his orange mongrel cat and constantly carried it around in his arms, petting it; and second, he was deathly afraid of flying. Although he had been relocated to the Midwest, he insisted on being driven to and from his trials against the mob in Rhode Island.

Red Kelley testified in a series of cases that put mobsters in jail. His prize testimony was against Raymond Patriarca in March 1970. The trial centered on the murder for hire of Rudolph "Rudy" Marfeo and Anthony Melei. Patriarca was charged with conspiracy to murder, along with Rudolph Sciarra, Luigi "Baby Shanks" Manocchio, John E. Rossi, Robert E. Fairbrothers, and Maurice "Pro" Lerner who was also indicted for the murder (a seventh defendant, Frank Vendituoli, had one of his charges dismissed and was found not guilty of accessory charge). Manocchio fled before the first trial so the case focused on the other defendants. All were convicted of conspiracy to murder and Lerner of murder and Raymond Patriarca was sentenced to ten years. Patriarca continued to run the mob enterprise from his cell. He completed his federal term in 1973 and was transferred to the Adult Correctional Institution in Rhode Island to begin his new stretch. Once paroled in January 1975 (an unusually short stint), Patriarca continued to rule with an iron fist until his death in 1984.

After the bulk of his testimony, John "Thomas" was re-located, we thought for good, to the Midwest. We had even shipped his furniture using our typical double-blind strategy: it was stored in a warehouse in Rhode Island under a marshal's name and shipped to one address; later it would go the real lo-cation. Thereafter, however, in 1983 Luigi Manocchio turned himself in to stand trial for conspiracy to murder. Law enforce-ment was puzzled as to why he did so but the reason became obvious when Red Kelley was summoned to Rhode Island as a witness against Manocchio. Kelley had developed some kind of dementia. The charges against Manocchio were dismissed based on Kelley's compromised mental state and some damaging ad-missions he would make on the stand.

In a subsequent application for post-judgment relief by Maurice "Pro" Lerner, he and the other defendants belatedly were exonerated. The Rhode Island Supreme Court concluded that Kelley had perjured himself during the Patriarca et al trial years earlier. In its decision the court also noted that the perjury was encouraged and corroborated by FBI Special Agent, H. Paul Rico, who himself committed perjury. Rico had handled Bar-boza's briefings on Thacher Island and Freshwater Cove. During my brief encounters with him, he acted like a wise guy. Despite these findings of his lying under oath and the reversal of the convictions arising out of the case Rico continued to be assigned to the Boston office. He would subsequently be implicated in another cover-up in the Deegan murder.

Red Kelley later died of natural causes.

10

RUNNING UP STOCKS

Back in the Wild West, when an old-time outlaw was asked why he robbed banks, he replied: "That's where the money is." The mob quickly realized, particularly with tutors like Vinnie Teresa, that the money was also in places other than banks; the newest reservoir of money was on Wall Street. The mob began to infiltrate the brokerage houses and made millions. One guy I protected who quarterbacked mob operations in the stock market was Michael Hellerman. He and his mob recipients were the precursors of the Enron crowd.

Michael Hellerman made millions for himself and his associates, and then the government came a calling. Hellerman could either spend the rest of his life in jail or become a protected witness. He chose the latter. By the time he finished testifying, he had helped put away dozens of hoodlums, brokers, swindlers, and businessmen who had been on his gravy train.

Significant organized-crime guys whom he brought down included John Dioguardi, a.k.a. Johnnie Dio, a soldier in the Thomas Luchese family; Carmine Traumunti, acting head of the Luchese crime family; Vincent Aloi, a capo in the Colombo family; Vincent Gugliaro; John Savino; Pasquale Fusco; Phil Bonodono; James Burkeson, son-in-law of Meyer Lansky; and Vincent Lombardo, along with wannabe higher-ups of the mob.

Hellerman's earlier career was pretty predictable. His father was a big-time banker, and Hellerman was highly educated and soon became a rising star on Wall Street. Had he stayed straight, he would have ended up a millionaire. Instead he became fascinated by the fast life of mobsters he saw from a distance. He wheedled himself into meetings with Crazy Joe Gallo and other hoods. Hellerman decided that instead of fronting his own money in any swindle he could use mob money and make himself a bigger profit. These connections would give him an in to the famous entertainers and sports figures of the day. Hellerman even got himself a mistress to parallel the lives of most wise guys.

One key swindle Hellerman would use was to control virtually all of a company's stock, but not own it all himself. Using mob money, he paid traders and brokers from various firms double what they would make on a stock commission to follow his lead on the stock manipulation. Hellerman would in effect control the stock of a shell corporation using nominees or phony names. The idea was to move the stock toward a prearranged price very gradually, say over six months. Hellerman knew that the Securities and Exchange Commission (SEC) would usually pick up only on a fast dump of shares.

If he bought Company X at a dollar a share, he'd move the price up to $25 a share by buying very small lots of shares at a higher price but his cohort brokers who were in on the deal would report a bogus volume of sales to create excitement for the trade for outsiders. Hellerman would also have them report "sales" at a higher price for shares he already owned at $1.00 The mob's $100,000 investment at a dollar of share to kick the scheme off was now "worth" $2.5 million. He would unload the stock at $25 or $30 per share by selling the stock to unsuspecting investors on his roster. He calculated that they would accept this failure as just a routine bad investment, given the ups and downs of the market, as long as their other stocks managed by Hellerman were doing well. Hellerman's fellow brokers did the same thing. They'd get a commission on top of the under-the-table—hence tax-free—payment, so they were ahead financially. Hellerman kept 10 percent, and the rest went to the mob.

Each transaction sought to make $3 million on the original $100,000 investment, minus expenses. Of course, there were dozens of phony stocks in play. Multimillions of dollars were made over the six-month period of manipulating the price. Greed, however, got the best of Hellerman. He began to move the stock in shorter periods: four months, and then three. This piqued the interest of the SEC, which initiated an investigation.

When the good times were rolling, Hellerman was living the high life. Sometimes he would borrow money from gang members, and then the noose would tighten when he couldn't repay it, and the "vig" (interest) would begin to toll. The Feds caught up with him over his shell corporation stock manipulation. In this scheme he's sold off stock to unsuspecting investors for a business that doesn't exist.

John Wing, chief of the Fraud Division of the U.S. Attorney's Office, requested security for him, which is how I met Michael Hellerman and his family. He was approximately forty years old and a bear of a guy. He was over six feet tall and out of shape. He sported kinky black hair and horn-rimmed glasses. You'd easily mistake him for a college professor. His then second wife was also tall, well-endowed, and pretty. The mob had arranged the marriage. Hellerman had liked Maria from the moment he met her when she was hatchecking at Michael's Steakhouse. Maria was full of life, almost boisterous. When I came into their lives, they had one child, a baby named Jennifer.

Upon my arrival to take them into protective custody, Hellerman spoke rapidly. My experience was that there was always somebody of whom these guys were deathly afraid. Vinnie

Teresa had been apoplectic about Joe Barboza bumping him off. Hellerman was afraid of Jimmy Blue Eyes, a.k.a. Vincent Aloi, a crime captain for New Jersey crime boss Gerardo Catena. Michael Hellerman found religion after he was out one night and two guys robbed his home. His second wife was there, and she sported an impressive rock. The hoods tried to wrangle it unsuccessfully from her finger. They then huddled and decided to chop off her finger to steal the ring. She apparently wailed so loudly that they left the house leaving her finger intact. Hellerman was convinced that he was the target for assassination that night; otherwise his wife would be down a digit. He owed a lot of vig on loans to the mob, so he decided to switch sides. He was familiar with the Witness Protection Program and thought it would keep him safe.

The first stop for Hellerman was federal court, where he was going to plead to securities fraud. I whisked him off to Rhode Island, and his wife and daughter were taken to an alternate location by another detail. After extensive debriefing with Bob Mondillo, who handled the prosecution, Hellerman changed his prior "not guilty" plea to "guilty" relating to the securities fraud counts that also implicated Dio and his crime family. There had been no threats on Hellerman's life prior to his plea, but his codefendants would know that he'd be testifying against them as soon as they learned of his guilty plea.

The marshals and I guarded every exit in the courtroom and the area immediately behind him at the time of his plea hearing. Because the court hearings are public, certain wise guys were there for the session. The deputy U.S. attorney took one look at the audience and asked Judge Morris Lasker for an audience in chambers. The U.S. attorney told me later that he explained to the judge what Hellerman was going to do and asked the judge to omit any reference to Hellerman's turning state's evidence during the plea, which had to be taken in public.

Inside the courtroom, I was aghast to hear the judge say partway through the proceedings: "You've shown a lot of courage admitting your wrongdoing and by helping the government by testifying." The wise guys in the benches turned white.

What an idiot, I thought to myself. While the mob would ultimately learn of Hellerman's change of heart, I had wanted at least a head start to get him out of Dodge. Hellerman received two years in jail and was ordered to make restitution based on his 10 percent of the ill-gotten gains from the investors he had swindled. He had no money to do so, but this would give the Feds a further hold on him until he paid it.

I hustled Hellerman out of a side door of the U.S. Attorney's Office in the courthouse. Later, my guys told me that the gang types ran to the pay phones to report to their bosses.

The defendants had millions of dollars tied into the schemes by that time and were connected to the Colombo and Luchese mob families. My office was requested to keep Hellerman near New York City because the trial was imminent and, given the complexity of stock fraud cases, Hellerman had to be available for consultation. He'd be one of the last witnesses to testify. We were requested to transport him to the U.S. Marshals Office in the Southern District of New York for the briefings because of the underground parking and access to the building.

Hellerman was nervous about being transported there. He told me a story about a deputy marshal in that office who was allegedly moonlighting at a job in a bar and was friendly with mobster Johnny Dio. I had no time to check out the veracity of the story and I wasn't going to take any chances, so I planned to have him debriefed at the U.S. Attorney's Office in the courthouse, where the moonlighter would never see him since his assignment was not at that location.

I also made the decision to return Hellerman to the Rhode Island safe house—the same one Vinnie Teresa had been in.

By this time, in 1970 and 1971, the place had eleven protected witnesses (sometimes up to seventeen) living there and twenty-four deputies who worked round the clock. It was a fortress. Even when an article appeared in the newspaper identifying the two-story farm as a safe house, I decided not to move the witnesses because I was confident in the security and the media did not know specifically who was being housed there.

Eventually the trial commenced against Johnny Dio and company, but not before Alan Dershowitz of Harvard Law School came to the trial to make noise about the lack of veracity of the witnesses. He was unsuccessful in derailing the trial, but he made Hellerman nervous. I dispatched two of my top deputies, Dennis Berry and Tony Anthony, to bring Hellerman to court. Two Southern District marshals, I would later learn, told my guys that the chief marshal of the Southern District wanted Hellerman to be brought to his office. My guys wisely declined in deference to the information regarding the moonlighting marshal.

At the commencement of the trial against the defendants, my marshals brought Hellerman into the chambers of Judge David Edelstein. He was solicitous of the witness's safety and urged Hellerman to tell him if there was anything he could do. Nervous Nellie Hellerman jumped at the chance. He recounted a story told to him by one of my protected witnesses in the Rhode Island safe house. This witness went to testify in a criminal case and saw an assassin sitting in the back of the courtroom. The marshals searched the guy, and, sure enough, he had two pistols. The assassin was dying of cancer so had nothing to lose; the mob had promised his family $50,000 if he carried out the execution. "I want everybody searched before they come into the courtroom," Hellerman requested. The judge complied with the request, with the exception of law enforcement and court personnel. This was before the high tech screening of today.

Dio and company were subsequently found guilty by the jury. While I was in the courtroom I thought that Hellerman came across as Professor Dudley-Do-Right, despite his deep involvement in the scheme.

In 1971 Hellerman took part in an undercover operation that netted Robert T. Carson, former aide to Republican Senator Hiram Fogg of Hawaii and then lobbyist from 1964–69 for payoffs during this period. At Carson's trial, U.S. deputy attorney general Richard Kleindienst testified that Carson had offered him $100,000 in contributions to the President Richard Nixon reelection committee in exchange for quashing the indictment against Hellerman in the Dio case. Kliendienst to my knowledge never clarified as to why Carson wanted to help Kellerman but I deduced that the real beneficiary was to be Johnny Dio when Carson pled guilty to charges he had attempted to quash the federal probe into the securities fraud case involving the gangster. Hellerman's involvement was to be merely the side show.

Hellerman returned to the safe house in Rhode Island to await his fate on his sentence for the Dio swindle. He was slapped on the wrist with a suspended sentence instead of the twenty large ones he could have been sentenced to because he had been an integral part of the scam. Eventually it was time to transition, and the process of giving him and his family a new identity began. Once completed, he would be on his own, since he obviously had the skills to be their breadwinner. By this time he had three children, so new social security cards had to be made, new birth certificates, drivers' licenses, and school records. Hellerman's mother lived at Surf Side in Miami, and Hellerman wanted to borrow money from her to reestablish himself. She was disgusted with the trajectory of his life of crime, but she ultimately relented, and he used the money to set himself up in the restaurant business. Hellerman opened four Cape Cod restaurants and then left one million dollars in bad debts in Massachusetts. He left his wife, Maria, behind in the Cape along with the debt. Hellerman met a girl, got her pregnant, and soon ditched her, too, in Massachusetts.

With a new name and a thriving restaurant in another part of Massachusetts, Hellerman met another girl from a prominent Massachusetts family. I even received an invitation to the wedding. I asked Hellerman if he had disclosed anything about his past, and he had not. I told him that I wanted to inform his soon-to-be in-laws, particularly since the bride was considerably younger than he was.

I arranged to meet the parents on Route 28, about ten miles from where Hellerman lived. While I didn't go into detail about his criminal past or disclose that he had been a guest of Uncle Sam in Witness Protection, I told them that he had a criminal record. I shared my knowledge that he was a consummate con man and had a violent temper. After I'd portrayed him as he was—namely, a guy who would rip off anybody—the parents were shocked. Nonetheless, the marriage went forward.

Witnesses react differently to being under protection and going into a new life. Michael Hellerman told me that what he found most difficult was giving up his family name. No grandchildren would bear the Hellerman name. It would pass into history (and not a great history, at that).

Hellerman, however, soon recovered from such nostalgia. Notwithstanding his book, *Wall Street Swindler: An Insider's Story of Mob Operations in the Stock Market*, which earned him a ton of dough, he nevertheless hankered for the good old days. He might have been planning a second volume, *From Wall Street to Flushing Queens Federal Savings and Loan Association*, because he continued to defraud people. Previously, Hellerman had written in his book about his scheme wherein he created a false identity using homemade social security cards.

With his gang of crooks, he would equip himself with a wig, makeup, glasses, and a false driver's identification and credit cards to back up the persona. Hellerman (or one of his accomplices) would then borrow $10,000 to $15,000 from a wise guy and take it to a bank to open an account.

After establishing himself as a construction executive, Hellerman would become friendly with the vice president of the bank. He'd wine and dine him and provide him with a prostitute who was introduced as his spouse. Her job was to seduce the banker and have an affair for up to six months in a lavishly appointed apartment. By this time the banker had been lulled into a false sense of security and would not check the bona fide background on his "friend" whose "wife" had become his paramour. The thief would then bring about $200,000 of stolen bearer bonds to the bank and Mr. Vice President would cash them. Then Hellerman would vanish with all of the money or his 75 percent split with his impostors. It would be weeks or months before the discovery that the bonds had been stolen. The banker would be able to provide only a phony business card of the thief. On occasion, if a picture was taken, the con man or Hellerman wasn't identifiable because of his disguise at the bank meetings. The tryst locale was emptied out.

Well, Michael Hellerman did not need to make up a false identity anew because I had provided him one through the U.S. Marshals Office. Using his new identification, Michael Rapp, he swindled the bank with very complicated schemes, leaving a trail of red ink for the savings and loan. Hellerman (Rapp) and his associates were eventually the targets of federal investigations for bilking banks in Los Angeles, Denver, Miami, and Orlando. In one case, Hellerman took a "loan" from Sun Bank of Miami in the amount of $1 million. He settled the dispute for $500,000.

Hellerman, a.k.a. Michael Rapp, used a coterie of people

up front on these schemes while he stayed in the background in order to bulletproof himself from any inquiries about his past. In 1986 a civil action ensued against Hellerman that accused him of taking a $30 million loan from the Florida Center Bank for a bogus project to finance the installation of pay phones along Florida's highways. Hellerman had allegedly drained $12.6 million before the bank's honchos realized that they weren't seeing any pay phones. Numerous Hellerman-controlled companies borrowed $1 million or more from banks. One such loan busted the Aurora Bank in Colorado when it wasn't repaid.

Hellerman and his associates were so audacious that they tried to buy a bank. The attempt faltered because of his and his associates' failures to pay back loans. Efforts to buy thrifts in Oklahoma and Tennessee also failed for the same reason.

Hellerman was indicted in 1987 and convicted for bank busting in Orlando, where federal auditors discovered $7.2 million in bad debts from 1985. Hellerman and his colleagues bought stock in Florida Center Bank and took out huge loans with worthless checks as collateral in the scheme to install pay phones. According to the twenty-three-page indictment, Michael's company, Pace-COM, had no employees, no staff, and no assets except for $800 in its corporate accounts. A codefendant was the chairman of the bank. Other codefendants included a pharmacist, a lawyer, a president of a money brokerage firm, and other purported sophisticated investors, who promptly blamed Hellerman for duping them. This indictment followed another one in Florida to defraud the Flagship National Bank of Miami, then subsequently Sun Bank, of $1 million. A closed Fort Lauderdale restaurant owned by him and his wife, Jane, was a front for the scheme. The restaurant's parent corporation was called Whatever, Inc. That certainly was his attitude.

Rapp was convicted in 1987 as the mastermind of the Florida

Center Bank caper and sentenced to thirty-two years. One of his codefendants became a fugitive. The others, whose lawyers referred to them as Hellerman's "windup toys," didn't convince the jury of their innocence. All were found guilty or pled guilty to the charges.

Hellerman also struck a plea bargain in the Sun Bank case and received a concurrent ten-year sentence that added no time to his overall sentence. Florida banking auditors nipped in the bud by two days a multimillion-dollar "loan in this case" Hellerman was charged in three other states. He rationalized his swindling by saying his problem was that he loved living high, gambling, and losing $200,000 a night.

Toward the end of his book on his swindling career, Hellerman wrote:

> *I would be less than candid if I told you that there aren't moments when I miss the night life, the excitement, the glamour of the entertainment world, Wall Street scheming, and even some of the people I dealt with in the mob. There have been times when I arrived in the community to live and work with strangers that I knew if I dared to chance it again I could pull off a swindle that could make me a rich man again. My success as a swindler, after all, was based on the greed and avarice of others, and wherever I've gone, I've found greedy people all looking to make a fast buck.[1]*

He added that the temptation was removed when he thought of prison or possible vengeance by those whom he testified

---

1. Michael Hellerman and Thomas Renner, Id., *Wall Street Swindler: An Insider's story of Mob Operations in the Stock Market,* 1977.

against. Apparently, his temptations grew too great—he was conning us again.

Hellerman's story clearly establishes one of the weaknesses of the Witness Protection Program. The fact that he was brilliant enough to make a great living without resorting to crime somehow convinced us that he would. Yet his taste of life on the "dark side" was too strong a pull for him. This nerd found a life of crime far more exciting than his former routine days.

Michael Hellerman, or Rapp, beat his "rap" in a way, since he got to serve it at Homestead Air Reserve Base in Florida, having convinced the judge that his life would be in danger in a regular prison. By the time you read this, he'll probably be out of prison. Watch your investments!

11

ANOTHER KIND OF
SOCIAL SECURITY

Some wise guys just have to "plan" for their retirement—with millions of dollars that Uncle Sam isn't supposed to know about. Take Gerald Zelmanowitz, who was a whiz at dealing with stolen securities. He'd get them from Joe Colombo, Meyer Lansky, and other top organized-crime bosses. The crime family would make extremely high-interest loans to security businesses' back-office staff. When a worker couldn't pay off, he was relieved of his debt by being forced to steal bearer bonds from the company's vault. The true owners wouldn't have a clue until it was far too late that the bonds had been purloined because they assumed their securities were under the proverbial lock and key at their brokers' offices.

In 1962, $1.3 million in negotiable securities walked out of the door of the brokerage firm Bache & Co. A stock record clerk, deeply in debt to the mob for a pony habit and fearful of cement shoes, had looked at his roster and found patrons who never checked on their bearer bonds, which are payable to "a bearer" as opposed to a specific individual. He tucked the bonds under his shirt and walked out of the building. Thus started a Wall Street joke: "When the Mafia talks, stock clerks listen." Sometimes bonds or stock certificates were obtained from customers' portfolios held at the institution. They would be purloined and forged by mobsters. These securities could be used as collateral for bank loans. The stolen securities would be stored in another bank vault while the loan proceeds, hundreds of thousands of dollars, marched out of the front door.

The mob itself ran neighborhood broker services. The mob guy would lock up the neighbors' treasuries, stock certificates, and bearer bonds in his safe. Shortly thereafter, the securities were off to the Cayman Islands for a tan. One such stealth caper occurred in the nineties, when General Motors Acceptance Corporation (GMAC) placed an order with American Banknote Corporation of Philadelphia to print a series of bearer bonds in $1,000 and $10,000 (Canadian) denominations and ship them to Chemical Bank in London. The printed bonds filled thirty-one cardboard containers. Somewhere between the printer's loading dock and the airport, one carton containing 1,500 bonds worth $7.9 million was stolen. The thief, Ronald Goldberg, was apprehended because GMAC acted fast in reporting the theft to the FBI, which found in Goldberg's possession some of the bonds he hadn't fenced yet.

Suffice it to say the mob had a good intelligence network of staff who had trouble paying the vig on their loans to the wise guys. With this repertoire of methods to get his hands on marketable securities, Zelmanowitz fenced millions of dollars in stolen or counterfeit securities, set up secret Swiss bank accounts, and cheated the government out of overseas investment taxes. He had an elaborate international securities shuffle scheme.

What brought Zelmanowitz into the Witness Protection Program in 1970 was his fear of getting plugged. Two vicious criminals from Newark New Jersey, Angelo "Gyp" DeCarlo and Daniel "Red" Cecere, approached Zelmanowitz to invest some money in partnership with another guy, Louis Saperstein.

Saperstein had a sticky-fingers problem and skimmed some of the money to pay off loan-shark debts. Saperstein ruefully concluded that DeCarlo and Cecere might kill him and decided to drop a dime on the men by writing "if" letters to the FBI—*if* Saperstein met his demise, DeCarlo and Cecere were the culprits. The FBI paid little attention to the missives until they discovered Saperstein's body with a belly full of arsenic.

Zelmanowitz was spooked. Earlier, he had been pinned against the wall at DeCarlo's office by a made man holding a butcher knife against his throat. Then he had witnessed Cecere and another man stomp Saperstein into a bloody pulp while demanding that he pay $5,000 every Thursday or he'd be dead. Saperstein's untimely death is what made Zelmanowitz ultimately turn to the authorities.

Before I got him as a charge, Zelmanowitz must have been a real charmer, or the FBI wanted the Newark hoods very badly, because he only got probation despite three indictments involving bank embezzlements and securities-related offenses. As a result of his testimony, DeCarlo and Cecere got twelve-year prison terms. DeCarlo got out a few months later when President Richard Nixon surprisingly commuted his sentence to time served. To this day I wonder whether DeCarlo was an informant.

Zelmanowitz and his wife, Lillian, were pretty demanding entrants into the witness Protection Program. Gerald Shur, a high-ranking justice official in charge of creating false identities, tried to make Zelmanowitz a retired sergeant in Army intelligence. Mrs. Z. took one look at the fake identity papers and threw them on the floor. No husband of hers would be a lowly sergeant! Despite Shur's trying to explain that this was only a cover and that the rank matched the fictitious background that had been created for them, she henpecked her husband into refusing the identity. Shur relented and made him a captain. Shur was beginning to pass out a lot of stripes!

After the Newark trial, my marshals whisked the family off to a motel in the nation's capital for initial relocation. I received a call sometime that night saying that somebody stole all the marshals' shotguns, ammunition, and walkie-talkies. I was not a happy camper. Because there was as much evidence that the marshals had been negligent and it was possible a third party had made off with the cache, nobody got punished except the guys on duty, who got a week's suspension.

The tribe of in-laws began to visit the Zelmanowitzes in Washington, D.C., despite the fact that the location was supposed to be under wraps. I ordered an investigation into how the information had gotten out, with a focus on Mr. and Mrs. as the chief culprits. I found no smoking gun.

Gerald Zelmanowitz's stepdaughter, Cynthia, got married in a real cloak-and-dagger wedding: guests were met near the now–Reagan Airport by a bus with U.S. marshals on it and brought to the Mayflower Hotel, where more marshals were waiting to guard it. Because the stepdaughter and her boyfriend had punctured the inner circle in finding the witness's whereabouts, Zelmanowitz wasn't allowed to know the new name given them after the nuptials. Zelmanowitz could communicate with her only by writing letters to the Justice Department, which would use a circuitous route to forward them to his daughter. She and her new husband enrolled at a university in California, feeling safe with their new identities. The Zelmanowitz's likewise went to college under an alias.

My office tried to get Zelmanowitz to move to the wide open spaces of Texas as his final relocation, but he and his wife nixed going to "Cowboyland." The couple insisted on San Francisco so they could be near the kids. The department relented; we had to unload the package because the program was mushrooming with new applicants.

Before departure, and in keeping with creating durable

background stories, I made arrangements for the marshals to drill Gerald and Lillian. The couple were driven to a suburb outside of Washington, D.C., and shown a house that they were supposed to commit to memory as their prior house. Later it was reported to me that Lillian made a snobby retort to Gerry Shur that she wouldn't be caught dead in such a pedestrian house. Little did she know it was actually Gerry Shur's house!

The Zelmanowitzes also had to study Gerald's resume for him to adopt as his own. He was allegedly born in Philadelphia, where he attended Bartram High School, followed by Baldwin-Wallace College in Berea, Ohio, and then served for twelve years in the Army Security Agency as a cryptographer. They had to know facts about the school and the town. Obscure places were chosen because it was unlikely that anybody would run into another Berean. For covers we looked for towns where people rarely moved away. Job selection was arranged so that the work experience would never result in, say, a neighbor asking for help from a supposed auto mechanic, leaving the witness without a clue as to what to do. Who would ask Gerry to encrypt something?

Before Zalmanowitz left for San Francisco, he tried to get his family relocated to Paris. Fearful that he wouldn't cooperate if needed because he was in another country, the Justice Department nixed the relocation. Only on rare occasions were protected witnesses allowed to relocate overseas. Zelmanowitz also tried to have Shur dissolve an IRS lien on a $104,000 brokerage account. When Shur told Zelmanowitz he had no power to do so, Zelmanowitz became livid.

Nonetheless, Zelmanowitz was grateful to have a second chance. Off they went to San Francisco, where they settled in as the Marises. Paul Maris's paperwork backed him up as the vice president and major shareholder of a company known as Sound Enterprises. Lillian would sometimes slip up and call him Jerry in front of people. Jerry had a tattoo with his name on his right bicep. The Justice Department sent him to the naval hospital for evaluation to see if it could be removed. Back then, it could not, so his new name became Paul J. Maris. If his wife slipped up or anybody saw it, he'd pass it off as his middle name.

Paul J. Maris began life anew as an insurance salesman making cold calls. One man he met had a failing garment business. Alvin Duskin took Maris into his confidence. Duskin had political ambitions and ran for some lower-rung positions with Maris serving as his campaign manager. When Duskin was elected, he turned his business over to Maris to run. Eventually, Maris bought the politician out and changed the name of his garment business to the Paul Maris Company. He focused on making Paul Maris one of the hottest labels for young women by taking ads out in the trendiest magazines of the time. Sales soared. Maris became a pillar of society, aiding the local Jewish charity fund-raising drives and setting up job fairs at Indian reservations. Maris got another company, Creative Capital, to invest $2 million in the company.

Maris stayed out of criminal trouble and was obviously relishing his new life. But the proverbial question remained: Can a leopard change its spots? In the case of Maris, the answer was: Somewhat. He continued to live high off the hog. His executive suite looked like a hotel's presidential suite. He leased a Rolls Royce. He couldn't get high living out of his system. Notwithstanding the fact that he had built this floundering company up to $8 million in sales, expenses for himself and the thirteen family members who were employed in the company resulted in no profit. Creative Capital became suspicious and decided to have him investigated. The thread of his garment industry was about to be pulled.

The Good Friday Massacre, when Maris was fired, happened on April 20, 1973. The board of directors of the Paul Maris

Company was shocked that even the workers in the factory who *weren't* Maris's relatives walked out in protest. The strike lasted a week before the board rehired Maris after he proffered that he would cut expenses. He did so, barely. Meanwhile, the chairman of the board, Milton Stewart, who also headed Creative Capital, was seething. He decided to hire a private eye, Hal Lipset, who had the reputation of always getting his man. Lipset initially checked Maris's background at the reported educational institutions. Uncle Sam had not managed to wall up those inquiries. While those facilities provided blank diplomas in cooperating with the government, because of inexperience Gerry Shur never told them they were for a Paul Maris, so he wasn't listed on the graduation roster. There was no birth certificate in Philadelphia. There was no listing of Maris as a retired army officer. When there was no record of Sound Enterprises, Lipset knew he was on to a phony.

A payroll clerk who had been preparing checks for severance after the first ouster also approached Stewart with a curiosity. Maris, his wife Lillian, and his clan working there all had sequential social security numbers! This was a big mistake that had been overlooked by the Social Security Service. Stewart sought and received a restraining order ousting Maris from his office. Maris reciprocated with a $5 million lawsuit, which only strengthened Stewart's resolve to find out who Maris really was.

With the initiation of the lawsuit, Maris's picture got in the newspaper and in the media. Soon a tipster said he looked like a guy in Newark, New Jersey, who used to be a swindler on behalf of the mob. Stewart dispatched people to Newark to search newspaper archives. Sure enough, Maris looked like an older version of Zelmanowitz. Zelmanowitz lost his lawsuit because of the misrepresentation on his application for borrowing money. Nobody would have lent him any money given his penchant for embezzlement.

In June 1973, while the marshals were asleep (this detail certainly had its problems!), Zelmanowitz and his wife stole out of the house and drove away. They lived under fictitious names at motels for about a month while staying in touch with the Justice Department, trying to negotiate a new deal.

On July 13, 1973, Zelmanowitz waltzed into the U.S. Senate with no protection to testify before the Senate Permanent Subcommittee on Investigations. Zelmanowitz complained about his blown alias. He said that the skills he learned as a criminal made him a successful businessman but that he never strayed into any criminal activities. He also implicated various local and federal officials whom he claimed were bribed by the mob.

Senator Henry Jackson was more interested in the machinations that had led to the release of Angelo Gyp DeCarlo. DeCarlo, a member of the Genovese crime family in New York, was an underboss who oversaw the family's loan-sharking operation. DeCarlo had been convicted earlier, in 1963, for paying bribes to New Jersey politicians, including New Jersey congressman Peter Rodino, Newark mayor Hugh Addonizio, and others. Senator Jackson believed that in DeCarlo's latest legal troubles, when he had been convicted of extortion related to the arsenic poisoning of Louis Saperstein, then–Attorney General Richard Kleindienst and recently White House counsel John W. Dean III, had bypassed normal procedures in processing executive clemency for DeCarlo after only one and a half years of a twelve-year sentence.

The senator wanted to nail then–Vice President Spiro Agnew, who was a buddy of DeCarlo and a suspected target for this abridgment of the sentence. He thought that Zelmanowitz would want to shed light on the matter, since DeCarlo was out of prison and potentially a threat to Zelmanowitz. There was some question in the proceedings as to whether Zelmanowitz had any information about laundering money for the Nixon campaign chest. The hearing didn't really establish anything. As abruptly as Zelmanowitz arrived, he left.

Having been finally ousted from his pinnacle, Maris made another play. On May 29, 1974, he sued the government for $8.35 million for each count for himself and $1 million up to $3 million for his spouse and family members who lost their jobs on the basis that they'd been given faulty aliases! He also sued to recoup $50,000 that he had put down on another business and forfeited because his associates learned of his background. He sued for mental distress. As far as I know, he didn't get a judgment.

Zelmanowitz did have some success, however, with another of his lawsuits. He sued the government over his tax problems. In a San Francisco federal court case, Judge Spencer Williams ruled on June 30, 1976, that he need not pay a multi-million-dollar tax liability. His argument was that he was merely an agent for the securities he had transported for DeCarlo and three others to investment banks abroad. He said he received no money from any of the investments on which the assessment was based. The court bought the argument.

He did get a new identity for himself and his family members, and they were all relocated somewhere in the United States. The last heard of him was when he flew first class to attend the wedding of Gary Bricker, the marshal whom I appointed to be in charge of guarding his life. At that time Zelmanowitz was trying to learn from the program and was constructing yet another identity which would be unknown to the government.

As for the marshals who lost their weapons and the ones who dozed off, let's just say I put them into another line of work as soon as I could.

12

HORSING AROUND

My protected witnesses used to regale me with stories about how the mob infiltrated legitimate businesses. If the entity made money, the mob was there to collect it. The schemes were ingenious. Legit motor-fuel distributors in New Jersey were driven out of business because mob-related enterprises didn't pay fuel taxes, thereby gaining a competitive edge. Need a tooth pulled? The mob siphoned off money from dental plans by posing as "consultants." Cigarette vending operations, "licensing boards" for gambling permits in Atlantic City, gambling schools, bars, restaurants, and hotels were all peopled by mob associates who gave participants their working papers and who would dutifully pay the mob back by skimming profits. The mob was the real party in interest in solid waste companies in the Atlantic states and would pump up the price of disposal through bid rigging. Electronic games of chance legitimately installed in New Jersey were manipulated so that the video games provided a steady source of income to the mob "winners." Nowhere, however, was the mob influence as pervasive in a supposedly legitimate business as in horse racing.

Of course, the mob was already getting the "juice" as loan sharks for those who had inveterate gambling problems. Along came a guy, however, who was the mob mastermind at fixing races. Anthony Ciulla's schemes filled the coffers of organized crime to the tune of millions of dollars, until he was tabbed for a sports-bribery conviction in New Jersey. As he got antsy cooling his heels in the can and after getting a tip that the infamous major Boston crime figure Howard T. Winter and his Winter Hill Gang were planning to ice him in a prison yard lest he be tempted to turn them in, he decided to pay back his ungrateful bosses. That brought me to the New Jersey prison where the FBI had moved him to solitary confinement to protect him from the yard.

Anthony Ciulla was the most unlikely brain trust to blow the whistle. Like Vinnie Teresa, he tipped the scales at over 350 pounds. At our first meeting, he was going stir-crazy in the little cell, since he took up practically the entire space with his girth. As with all intakes of candidates for the program, I did a profile on him. He had never finished high school and talked like a "dem and dose" hood, even though he was extremely smart. He had his own gambling problem and often flew to one state or another to implement his race-fixing on behalf of the Boston mob. He loved his then–twelve-year-old daughter, his wife, Helen, and even his mother-in-law, for whom he also wanted protection. Because he was serving a five-year sentence at the time, with another sentence awaiting him in Rhode Island, there was no chance he would get out of incarceration—at least, not until he produced results.

I made arrangements to move him into federal custody because of regulations that required this move. Those plans were aborted when the extent of the Winter Hill Gang influence became apparent. No jail location was safe, including our usual stand-by, a facility in New Hampshire. Inmates at the Rhode Island Adult Correctional Institution, looking for some time to be clipped off their sentences, had informed the Rhode Island State Police that they had been told to murder Ciulla if he arrived there. His size would make him stand out like a target anywhere, so I moved him initially to the Massachusetts Police Barracks.

During that move, there was already a bounty on his head, including instructions from Howard Winter himself to plug any agent who got in the way. This assignment was particularly dangerous for my guys, since Ciulla had to be transported daily for debriefing by Massachusetts authorities, who were salivating to arrest Winter, who had financed the race-fixing, and two of his top lieutenants, John Matarano and Joseph McDonald, who were on the FBI's Ten Most Wanted fugitive list. Since the race-fixing scheme reached into Detroit, Rhode Island, and New Jersey, I had to make arrangements for his transport to these locations as well. Part way through the debriefing trips, we learned that the gang might have received information as to the location of Ciulla at the police barracks, so I moved him to a naval facility in Massachusetts that was about five minutes away from the courthouse for his grand jury and trial testimony.

This assignment was going to be treacherous for about a year as we learned information as to the ever-escalating bounty on Ciulla's head. A witness who was living in California had been shot and murdered in the garage of his home in the presence of his wife because they thought he was a canary singing against McDonald. (He wasn't.) Nobody at that time knew where McDonald was, so we were on the alert in case he made an appearance to pop Ciulla.

The stakes were very high for Winter. He and his boys had lived a charmed life, one step ahead of authorities, and this investigation, with Ciulla as the star witness, threatened to bring down Winter's whole operation. At one point, Ciulla's sister told Ciulla that she had been called on by a Winter Hill Gang member and told that if Ciulla ever testified against Winter or any of his associates, Ciulla would be attending funerals for the rest of his life for members of his family until his own inevitable murder. She, too, got protection.

Ciulla's cooperation with the New Jersey attorney general resulted in seventy indictments being returned. Again, a furious Winter, clearly the most important organized-crime figure in Boston after La Cosa Nostra boss, Gennaro Angiulo, ordered all of his henchmen to exhaust every avenue to find Ciulla and kill him.

Indictments were handed down in 1979 against Winter and five members of his gang. Ciulla had to be kept under wraps for the forty-five-day trial, in which all of them were convicted by a jury. Even then, Ciulla stayed in protection, since the defendants appealed the convictions in 1980 on all forty-two counts on which they were found guilty. Ciulla was an unindicted co-conspirator and had received immunity for his testimony against his confreres. All the convictions were sustained on appeal except for two defendants who got off on a technical mistake made by the prosecution. Ciulla was then placed in permanent relocation with his family.

In case you are as curious as I was about how Ciulla fixed the races, here's what he told me—nonstop for about an hour. Quite simply he would bribe jockeys (sometimes with chump change of $500 to $1,000), trainers, owners, and racing officials up and down the East Coast to prevent specific horses from finishing in the top three positions in a given race. Sometimes the payoff was cocaine or hashish instead of cash. If they hesitated or failed to perform as directed, Winter would muscle them with violence to comply. Illegal offtrack bookmakers throughout the country were used to place the bets, so this scheme ripped off other bad guys as well. Several guys on the Winter payroll would purchase large quantities of perfecta, exacta, trifecta, or quinella tickets on the fixed races. Legitimate bookmakers throughout New England and Las Vegas would also be used, but they would not know about the fixed races. Huge winnings were brought back to Motorama Sales, Inc., a Massachusetts dealership owned by Winter, who would take 50 percent of the winnings and divide the other 50 percent proportionately among the confederates.

To spread more money around, the players decided to purchase a horse called Spread the Word. The jockey would hold it back so it performed miserably for several races. One time, he told me, a suspicious steward questioned the jockey about the poor showing of the steed. In order to avoid that risk again, the jockey would have Spread the Word gallop for a mile or two before a race so as to exhaust it. When the odds were high enough, the horse was entered with inferior steeds and allowed to win. At one point this gambling enterprise was raking in so much money that it had to be laundered, so the participants bought the Squire Lounge, a topless go-go joint in Revere, Massachusetts.

Ciulla testified at trial that it was his idea to fix these races. He met with Winter at a bar called, fittingly enough, the Back Room where it was decided that he'd deal with the jockeys and trainers. Once he had found sufficient takers of the bribes, he'd notify Winter as to which race would be fixed the next day. The syndicate would know ahead of time the horses to be held back and the one that would win. Tickets for the "winners" would be purchased just before the post time.

Folks outside the mob have often heard about the proverbial brown bag full of money. Ciulla used brown lunch bags to pack tens of thousands of dollars per race winnings. He was the bagman in the fullest sense of the term.

As for Winter, his conviction on the race-fixing case effectively removed him from the leadership of the Winter Hill Gang. Upon his release, he was subsequently convicted on drug charges and spent another decade in jail. As to "what goes around, comes around" the FBI gave him a chance to duck the charges and sentence if he testified against Whitey Bulger, but he refused since, in his words, he wasn't a rat. To my knowledge he is currently living in Massachusetts.

Ciulla disappeared into the woodwork after my contact with him. I don't know what happened to him subsequently. His cover was apparently so deep after his relocation that only the need-to-know bosses kept tabs on him.

13

BURGLARS AND BUNGLERS

E. Howard Hunt arrived wearing his trademark hat with a wide brim pulled over his eyes. For his role in Watergate—putting together the team of infiltrators at the Democratic National Committee—Hunt had earned a thirty-three-month sentence. It was late in the day when I introduced myself. Hunt promptly asked for a "broad" for the night. I told him the U.S. Marshals Service didn't provide *that* service. Hunt emitted a sound that communicated disgust. Nonetheless, he quickly adopted the posture of a "brother"; he had been in law enforcement too, and he broke the ice by asking us about our jobs.

A graduate of Brown University in my home state of Rhode Island, Hunt served in the Navy and, starting in 1949, the CIA. In Mexico he was station chief and implemented the plan to overthrow Jacobo Arbenz Guzmán, the elected president of Guatemala. This success earmarked him as the strategist to put together a Cuban government in exile that would be placed in office after the ouster of Fidel Castro. The operation's failure undermined his career in the CIA, but Hunt emerged as an operative in Nixon's inner circle.

Hunt's first assignment for Nixon was to break into the Los Angeles office of psychiatrist Dr. Lewis Fielding to steal the files on Daniel Ellsberg. Ellsberg had leaked the so-called Pentagon Papers, which gave an unfavorable picture of the war in Vietnam. Hoping to discredit Ellsberg, the Nixon administration planned to leak his mental health problems to the press. No Ellsberg files were found, probably because Fielding was extra-cautious; he had earlier refused an FBI request for the data on Ellsberg. The break-in was initially undetected.

The go-to man for Republican operatives, Hunt was asked to dig up dirt on Edward Kennedy, then a potential presidential candidate prior to the 1969 Chappaquiddick scandal.[1] Hunt knew of my relationship with Bobby Kennedy and got a kick out of trying to get a reaction from me when he ragged against Bobby's brother Ted. Hunt was the master of disinformation. According to the *New Yorker's*[2] Seymour Hersh, Nixon and Charles Colson, the White House counsel and Nixon's hatchet man sent Hunt to the home of Alabama governor George Wallace's assailant, Arthur Bremer, to plant George McGovern campaign brochures in order to link the attack on Wallace to a fan of the Democratic presidential hopeful. Such a link would mortally wound McGovern in the South because many southerners supported Wallace. Hunt also masterminded Nixon's "Plumbers," a unit in the Nixon White House that ferreted out the internal sources of unfavorable news leaks regarding the Vietnam War effort. Hunt was then tapped to execute the burglary at the Democratic National Committee headquarters, which took place on June 17, 1972.

Howard Hunt began to feel the cold shoulder of President

---

1. Mary Jo Kopechne was found dead in a car in Chappaquiddick, Massachusetts, a day after it crashed into the river. Edward Kennedy had been the driver and had swum to safety, leaving the scene of the accident.

2. "A Reporter at Large" by Seymour M. Hersh, *New Yorker*, December 14, 1992.

Nixon when the operation was bungled. He apparently demanded a different kind of "hush money" to stay quiet about the genesis of the operation, which led back to the White House—he wanted his records at the CIA cleansed of any negative entries. Nixon's gang made a preemptive strike, marginalizing him by portraying him as a renegade operative who had no contact with the White House in committing this folly.

Indicted on September 15, 1972, on bugging charges, conspiracy, and burglary, Hunt pled guilty without a flinch on January 11, 1973. With the Watergate hearings scheduled for May 17 to August 7, 1973, he was placed in our program for protection in the meantime.

Hunt wasn't forthcoming about his own escapades; he wasn't exactly Mr. Talkative when interviewed by the FBI regarding its own conduct of the Watergate investigation and by the Senate committee prosecutors. The FBI had been roundly criticized (including its acting head, L. Patrick Gray, and its former bosses, Attorneys General Mitchell and Kleindienst) for capitulating to the White House's demands to tune down the inquiries. Hunt seemed to scoff at the FBI's lack of guts. As for the prosecutors, Hunt hated Fred Thompson (who would run for president in 2008). Hunt thought Thompson was an actor long before he became famous for his stint on the *Law and Order* shows! Hunt mentioned in passing that he wasn't interested in giving the Senate crowd any preview before he was called to testify. The agents certainly seemed frustrated with him after debriefings. I actually thought Hunt would eventually refuse to testify, even to the Watergate committee.

Hunt was a man's man. He wasn't demanding at all and regarded complaining as something crybabies do. However, Hunt did confide that he was worried about his mounting legal expenses. Not paying his bills really bothered him, since welching on debts, even to lawyers, was not a stand-up thing to do.

He eventually filed for bankruptcy years later. Hunt considered himself one of the "good guys"—a patriot—and expected to be treated with respect. He'd play cards for hours with the marshals on duty and requested cigars, which we got for him. Hunt felt very comfortable in our presence, and we treated him as a "brother," too. Occasionally, he'd lapse into musing that all patriots have to take their lumps and do unpleasant things for national security. Hunt would comment that although he might not be remembered that way, what he had done was for the good of the United States.

A couple of my marshals tried to pry information from the taciturn Hunt. There was plenty of gossip that he knew who was behind the slaying of John F. Kennedy. He never directly made any accusations but obliquely referenced the CIA and Lyndon Baines Johnson. Badly damaged by the Bay of Pigs fiasco, the CIA in turn blamed JFK for a lack of guts in rejecting a Cuban invasion to oust Castro. Hunt made no bones about the fact that he felt JFK was too faint of heart in pulling the punches on the mission and said JFK probably got what he deserved since he wasn't a leader at all.

One day a marshal asked Hunt point-blank about whether he was in Dallas the day of the Kennedy assassination. Hunt smiled and said he'd leave that inquiry to the history books. He added, though, that far too many intelligence operatives couldn't find their butts with their hands, so maybe history wouldn't unravel what really happened. He suggested that he might need to put his two cents in later on. Subsequently, Hunt gave a classified statement to the House Select Committee on Assassinations, which was investigating the killing of JFK. Articles and books were rife with the contention that he had acknowledged to the committee his and CIA involvement. While he wasn't under our wing at the time, I only know that the man preferred to be enigmatic, and I just couldn't picture him making such a clear statement. If true, he would probably want to break the news himself and not through some committee. While he had a respect for the chain of command, Hunt felt skeptical as to whether it was operating correctly in D.C.

Hunt made a lot of money writing dozens of spy novels under various pen names—apropos given his CIA background. I surmised that his use of pseudonyms wasn't because he was abashed at writing under his own disgraced name as much as it was that he was pulling the leg of the reader as to who really penned the novel.

Howard Hunt's wife, Dorothy, was killed in the December 8, 1972, crash of United Airlines Flight 553 in Chicago. Various federal agencies, including Congress, investigated the crash and found it to be an accident occasioned by crew error. Her body was found in the wreckage along with her pocketbook with $10,000 cash in one-hundred-dollar bills. Rumors duked it out as to whether she was trying to escape from Howard to start a new life or was really his bagman siphoning off funds to start a new life with him.

Following his father's death, young Saint John Hunt gave an interview to *Rolling Stone*[3] with an alleged deathbed confession by the elder Hunt of his involvement in the assassination of JFK at the behest of the CIA and then–Vice President Lyndon Johnson. I suppose history will have to sort that out. I always wanted to read his spy novels, which I was sure were all together truly his autobiography. Maybe I'll get around to that and find out what really might have happened in Dallas that day.

• • •

3. "The Last Confessions of E. Howard Hunt" by Erik Hedegaard, *Rolling Stone*, April 05, 2007.

While men dominated the Watergate news, I was struck by how much their wives were like their "sisters" in the mob. Attorney General John Mitchell had perhaps the only spouse who wasn't centrally cast as the adoring wife; Martha Mitchell was referred to as the "mouth who roared" because of her whistle-blowing on the activities of her husband and the Nixon crowd. More typical was Maureen Dean, John Dean's dutiful wife. My job was to protect Maureen and John for his appearance before the Senate Watergate Committee from June 25 to June 28, 1973, and afterward. The Deans remained in the program because he was also a witness in the Mitchell-Stans trial. Mitchell and Maurice Stans, the secretary of commerce, were charged with, among other things, conspiracy to impede the Securities and Exchange Commission's investigation of Robert L. Vesco, a fugitive at the time of the spring 1974 trial, in return for a cash contribution of $200,000 to Nixon's reelection campaign. The men were acquitted. According to posttrial interviews, while the jurors were impressed with Dean's rapier mind, they were put off by his admission that he was awaiting sentencing on his plea of guilt regarding conspiracy to obstruct justice. They thought he was out to save his own skin.

Maureen was engaged to John at the start of the Watergate scandal and she married him shortly thereafter. He was the White House Special Counsel to President Nixon from July 1970 to April 1973, when Nixon fired him upon learning that he was singing to investigators. Nixon regarded him as a turncoat who was peddling lies.

There's no question that Dean was deeply involved in events leading up to Watergate. He and his soon-to-be fellow felons blamed each other as the masterminds. Despite eschewing such a key role, Dean was front and center at all the important meetings involving the cover-up by the FBI of its conduct of the investigation of the Watergate burglary. John Mitchell was the attorney general, and the indictment of his conduct was that the FBI pulled its punches instead of rooting out the miscreants of Watergate at his direction as the agency's ultimate boss. On November, 1973 Dean pled guilty to obstruction of justice before Watergate trial judge John Sirica. He admitted supervising payments of hush money to the Watergate burglars, notably Howard Hunt, and he outlined the so-called enemies list maintained for the president, who sought dirt on those opposing him. Dean's sentence was finally handed down some nine months later: one to four years in a minimum-security prison. By the time of sentencing, he had completed the testimony before the Senate Watergate Committee but not the seminal trial against Watergate conspirators John Mitchell, H. R. Haldeman, John Erlichman, Robert Mardian, and Kenneth Parkinson, which concluded on January 1, 1975.

On September 3, 1974, Dean was diverted to me and the U.S. Marshals Service for protection at Fort Holabird near Baltimore. His sentence would later be reduced by Judge Sirica to nine months, which Dean actually served in the safe house so he could be debriefed by the prosecutors for the pending conspiracy trial.

Subsequently, former attorney general John Mitchell was found guilty of conspiracy, obstruction of justice, and perjury. Faced with a potential thirty years, he received a reduced sentence of one to four years. He served nineteen months of his sentence.

H. R. Haldeman, Nixon's White House chief of staff, was convicted of conspiracy and obstruction of justice. Notwithstanding the potential of twenty-five years in prison, he was sentenced to an eighteen-month prison sentence plus a $16,000 fine.

John Erlichman, Nixon's assistant on domestic affairs, was convicted of similar charges with a penalty similar to Haldeman's.

Robert Mardian, aide to Mitchell, was also convicted. His

attorney was sick during the trial, so the conviction was overturned, and he was never retried.

Kenneth Parkinson, legal counsel for the Committee to Re-Elect the President was acquitted.

It was interesting to follow Maureen's and John's ups and downs as attacks escalated by Republican officeholders like then U.S. Senator Hugh Scott and Nixon White House operatives and as verdicts were reached. John tried to maintain a stoic face on the roller-coaster ride. When Nixon finally agreed to release the tapes made in the White House of the relevant meetings, Dean focused correctly on the fact that they tended to support his testimony before the committee. They also, however, reinforced his position as more than just a bit player. He sounded like the leader in making sure the cover-up was just that until after the election against Democrat George McGovern and then advising Nixon on how to maintain the stonewalling as the cover-up broke.

Almost from the first day it was known that Dean was going to testify in a way contrary to the president's wishes, the Deans' reputations were attacked. The swirling rumors made for a very tense relationship between the Deans. These rumors—that the break-in of the Democratic National Committee was really orchestrated by Dean to retrieve pictures of his then-call girl fiancée, Maureen, who was servicing "leading Democrats"—really frosted the couple's relationship. Watergate-implicated principal G. Gordon Liddy made these claims later in his book, *Will: The Autobiography of G. Gordon Liddy.* The Deans promptly sued and subsequently claimed that there was a settlement in their favor. In any event, the couple was caught between a rock and a hard place, since the story was nebulous and they had a fear of promulgating it beyond a tight circle by going on the offensive.

Maureen looked the part of such rumors. At the age of twenty-five, she sat like a porcelain figure at the hearings. This former stewardess, the daughter of a onetime Ziegfeld chorus girl, carried herself with an air of royalty. She had been married twice and was considered a swinger because of the nightclub crowd she hung around with. She was the perfect target for such stories.

Maureen would make certain comments that revealed her naïveté. She once mentioned that her husband's job was cloaked in attorney-client privilege with the president, so she knew not to ask John any questions. In our presence, the Deans rarely discussed anything about his testimony or role, and it wasn't our job to pry.

John Dean was no problem whatsoever in the program. He was easy come, easy go. I'd usually talk sports or police work with him. He knew that the marshals would work out the schedule so that he wouldn't run into John Mitchell or any of the other defendants who had court appearances on a variety of pretrial matters. My biggest worry was that some nut would try to kill him. It wasn't like the mob trying a hit—more like protecting him from the people who gunned down Governor Wallace or the Kennedys. Protecting a witness from a mob hit is somewhat easier because there is intelligence, culled from the FBI investigations and the witness himself, on who might gun down the principal. In the case, however, of somebody who is unhinged going after your charge, there is much more of a random factor, and it's more difficult to protect the person.

Sometimes it was important to get people out of the safe house because of the tension surrounding them. There was plenty of that during the Watergate hearings and the subsequent trials. One of the most experienced marshals, Donald "Bud" McPherson, was guarding the Deans for a while. He noticed that they were really reaching a boiling point and asked what he could do. After consultation the couple decided that they wanted to go to the Grand Ole Opry, the bastion of country music in Nashville, Tennessee. At first, Bud demurred; 85 percent of people polled had said they watched the Watergate proceedings at some point on television, and John Dean had been a nonstop participant for several days. John was in Nashville going over his testimony with a prosecutor earlier in the day. Bud wasn't thrilled but he decked them out with floppy hats and sunglasses. The concern, of course, was for a Lee Harvey Oswald–type takeout, but the air was also rife with potential CIA retribution. One of the theories in the President John F. Kennedy assassination was that the CIA might have been involved, and E. Howard Hunt, who was on the hot seat for the Watergate scandal, was a former CIA guy whom Dean was implicating in wrongdoing. At the Opry, nobody noticed John Dean, but when the couple wandered into the Opryland Amusement Park, they began to attract attention.

John got jittery. "These guys are staring at me," he whispered to Bud. The guys were staring, Bud would recount to me, but it wasn't at John. They were staring at Maureen, who was decked out in a tight sweater. Since Bud didn't want to be there anyway, he quickly shepherded the couple out.

Maureen was always nice. She tried to keep a cheerful face, but the pressure would sometimes make her cry. While she had an air of sophistication about her, she also showed that she was very grateful for all the efforts made by the marshals. The hardest time for her was when John did go to prison for four months of his sentence. The most serious I ever saw him was when the jail door clanked in front of him. He was kept from other prisoners for his own safety.

After the Watergate matter ran its course, I thought that the threat against the Deans had abated. There was no need to change their identity. I understand that they are still together today and living in California. They had to be the politest couple we ever had in the program.

14

THE MOB'S PIGGYBANK:
UNION PENSION FUNDS

The mob usually had an easy entrée into the unions. Joe Teitelbaum, owner of a Miami stevedoring company, played ball with organized crime. On the Atlantic and Gulf coasts, the International Longshoremen's Association (ILA) ripped off shipping lines, stevedores, small businesses, and foreign countries as it lathered campaign contributions onto politicians. The racketeers sold labor peace on the docks, where delays could cost shipowners $35,000 per day.[1] If a shipowner didn't pay, he was inundated with rigged bids on ship repairs, orchestrated workers' compensation claims, and cargoes fingered for truck hijackers. Virtually everybody coughed up the cash.

Teitelbaum, a five foot four inch powerhouse, was relatively successful but eventually got fed up with the system of bribes, graft, extortion, kickbacks, and "rent." His handlers got too greedy: they scared off Teitelbaum's customers when he fell behind in payments, and then, in 1975, he had a bad scare with heart disease. The combination of these events turned him to the FBI, and he agreed to wear a wire.

Teitelbaum got some big scores and also helped FBI agents

---

1. In 1970 U.S. dollars.

infiltrate the labor rackets. From 1977 to 1986 he helped convict fifty-two union officers and fifty-eight company executives and corporations. The big fish he landed included ILA's number three officer, Anthony Scotto, boss of Brooklyn Local 1814. The FBI's electronic surveillance provided evidence that Scotto was a capo in the Gambino family. The Gambino syndicate controlled the docks as far south to Norfolk, Virginia with the Genovese gang from New York controlling the waterfront with ILA locals farther south of Norfolk. These convictions gained with Teitelbaum's cooperation, showed that four unions—the International Brotherhood of Teamsters (IBT), the ILA, the Hotel Employees and Restaurant Employees International Union (HERE) and the Laborers International Union of North America—were marinated in organized crime.

Representing three million workers, labor leaders like George Barone, William Boyle, James Vanderwide, and Fred Field bit the dust. Scotto was convicted despite character references from then New York Governor Hugh Carey and former Mayor John Lindsay, whose favorable opinions no doubt were the result of all those union votes and contributions. In fact, the Bad Four unions contributed $4.7 million during the election cycle to favored Congressional candidates and the election committee of President Jimmy Carter who subsequently invited Scotto to dine at the White House.

My job brought me in contact with Teitelbaum on October 21, 1977. The Justice Department had received information that he was to be killed in order to nip in the bud the burgeoning federal investigation of unions' mob activities. Six weeks earlier, on September 1, 1977, the *New York Times* had run a front-page article that fingered Teitelbaum as an informant with, as we say in law enforcement, his name, rank, and serial number.

Despite all the media exposure, Teitelbaum refused to leave

his home for another point of safety. He ignored his predicament in the name of normalcy for his wife and five children, proceeding with such daily activities as attending parents' meetings at his son's high school and preparing for his college-aged daughter's marriage. The Justice Department was flipping out over the fact that he would not leave his home in Miami. Were he to get rubbed out, not only would the trials be jeopardized, but also other witnesses would get cold feet.

Three days after my superiors briefed me about my Teitlebaum assignment, I personally met Joe at a motel not too far from his residence. He promptly peppered me with comments about how he shouldn't have to run—let the bad guys run instead. I proposed a deviation from our usual protection program, in which the principal and family are moved to a safety zone. Instead, I outlined a plan for protection at his house, using eight men on a regular schedule. My proposal would start his protection using eight marshals and gradually downsize from eight guys to six, four, then two, based on intelligence and on an assessment of the threat, and eventually down to a spot check after all the trials, since the threat would then be reduced. He agreed that this was a fair proposal.

I perceived my role with him to be nothing but security, although I did suggest to him that he testify before a congressional committee since he had intimate knowledge of organized crime and its control of the docks. Subsequently, in February 1981, the Senate Permanent Subcommittee on Investigations did hear from Teitelbaum. In addition to the testimony he served up on the mob, he also raised serious questions about commitments made to him by the Witness Protection Program. I reported what I knew, namely, that a security lapse involving him had occurred on the day the grand jury returned indictments and that excessive amounts of money were spent on the detail when the Justice Department jiggered with my plan.

Eventually, the protection plan was lambasted for spending close to $2 million to protect Teitelbaum and his family.

The use of his testimony resulted in arguably the most successful racketeering probe the FBI had ever mounted. I had to wonder, however, whether all avenues were truly exhausted to root out mob influences in unions. Politicians couldn't wrap their arms tight enough around union leaders with mob ties because of their campaign contributions and ability to move voter blocks. There certainly is a lack of political will to fight the war on this type of corruption.

Roy Williams, head of the IBT, whose 1.9 million members ranged from airline pilots to truck drivers, testified that his union had been under the thumb of organized crime for three decades. He went on to say that every major teamster local had some connection with organized crime and that his successor, Jackie Presser, was "as controlled as I was."

FBI Director William Webster noted that a racket tariff was imposed on all goods shipped through U.S. ports. Syndicate-managed thefts at the Miami port alone totaled $2 billion a year, which, he noted, was passed on to consumers. The 400,000 members of HERE saw the union's assets of $21.4 million shrink to less than $14 million through "loans" to gangsters and associates. Studies show that construction costs in New York City are 20 percent higher than they should be because suppliers have to buy marked-up materials from mob businesses.

In New Jersey, mafia boss Tony Provenzano ruled a Teamster local by sheer terror. In his Local 560, two members who dared to oppose him were plugged. He made businesses hire ghost employees and let companies be forced into bankruptcy through inside thefts. When he was finally sent to prison, he put his brothers in charge and ruled the Teamsters from his cell. He finally caught life imprisonment for murder. His "elected" successor as the local's secretary-treasurer was his twenty-three-year-old daughter. Nepotism is the rule, not the exception.

Union leaders have even lobbied to cut the Justice Department division that oversees pensions. I used to ask myself whether company owners like Joe Teitelbaum ever wondered if it was worth it to go up against corrupt unions.

Another informant I protected was Ralph Picardo. In the fall of 1975, while he was in the New Jersey State Prison in Trenton, he notified federal authorities that he had information regarding the disappearance of Teamsters boss Jimmy Hoffa. He was removed from prison using a writ of habeas corpus filed on his behalf to protect him.

Picardo offered to provide information without any commitment from the government until the government was completely satisfied as to the truthfulness and accuracy of his information. At the time he was under a sentence for conspiracy to commit murder. Picardo then launched into a recitation of a decade's-worth of crime by the Anthony Provenzano crime group. He particularly addressed Provenzano's scheme to obtain a loan of several million dollars from the Utica (New York) Teamsters Benefit Fund, ostensibly for the renovation of a Manhattan hotel but actually to generate kickback money for the 10 percent to his co-conspirators joining him in looting the fund.

On July 11, 1978, Provenzano was convicted and sentenced to four years. Meanwhile, another indictment was handed down against Provenzano and Local 560 official Anthony Castellito. With Picardo's testimony, Provenzano received a sentence of life imprisonment.[2] Provenzano got whacked with another indictment courtesy of Picardo. On February 22, 1979,

---

2. The conviction was reversed on procedural grounds but was reinstated by the New York Court of Appeals.

Provenzano and four associates were tagged with another rack-eteering charge—in return for "labor peace," Seatrain Lines in Weehawken had paid them about $250,000 in order to use non-union help. All were convicted.

Ralph Picardo wasn't done with the Provenzano family. Nunzio Provenzano, Tony's brother and the heir-apparent while Tony was in jail was also indicted on the basis of Picard's infor-mation. Nunzio and others had demanded and received huge payments from officials of four trucking companies in exchange for "labor peace." Eventually, all were convicted and jailed.

Other witnesses, including Nelson Lee Pierson, Charles Musto, Mike Sciarra, and John DeStephano, were also given protection from the Provenzano operation. Pierson was a union delegate for Local 560, and the others were all collectors for loan-shark operations. These guys sought witness protection after Samuel Guidotti, president of Local 35, had a hearing be-fore Judge Lawrence Whipple, a U.S. District Court judge, on July 17, 1973. Guidotti was seeking to have his sentence ended because of his "heart problems." A fellow prisoner who had given him mouth-to-mouth resuscitation reported that Guidotti wanted to get out of prison to destroy union loan-shark records.

A member of Provenzano's crime family in jail at that time, Sal Briguglio, paid the prisoner in the next cell $40,000 to do hits on these witnesses. Charles Musto reported that a crime family member had approached him to say that he'd be ap-proached by the FBI and that if he did not do the right thing, he and his family would be killed. Guidotti remained in prison, and all these men were protected by the program. Their information resulted in successful prosecutions.

Picardo's information on Jimmy Hoffa did not bear fruit. Be-cause of the accuracy of his other information and the resulting convictions, many former Justice Department officials think his information on Hoffa was correct even though it could not be corroborated. All the suspects have since died, and the feeling of the Justice Department was that justice had been served because all of those implicated by Picardo were successfully prosecuted and sentenced to substantial terms of imprisonment.

When I guarded Picardo, he told me that he felt he had made a great contribution, and not just with the convictions of the bad guys. His revelations of the dynamics of organized crime's infiltration of labor unions and the trucking and shipping industries provided the basis for law enforcement's dramatic policy changes.

Picardo's cooperation did not result in his release immediately from incarceration. He remained in a jail-like facility under conditions which were tantamount to solitary confinement. This became the norm rather than the exception. Ironically, Picardo finally had his own conviction reversed in 1977, yet he stayed around to brief the government on other schemes and to participate in trials. Of all the people I met, he seemed most sincere about reversing his life of crime and doing something good. As far as I know, he is alive with a new identity. I hold a lot of respect for his courage.

In case you think that the Witness Protection Program was only for men, think again. When I first took Annette Gilly into custody, she was in jail, charged with conspiracy to kill coal miners union leader Joseph Jock Yablonski and his wife and daughter. She had been incarcerated from September 1971 through March 1972.

Annette Gilly decided to testify as a key witness in the conspiracy murder trial of against her father, Silous Huddleston, and her husband, Paul Gilly and other accomplices. Paul was ultimately convicted of the Yablonski murders and eventually sent to death row. Her testimony would also convict her father, who escaped execution because his bad health caught up with him first. They certainly weren't a *Little House on the Prairie* kind of family. Six trials stretched over 4 years in three jurisdictions.

Annette Gilly was removed from the prison and put into protection when she also offered to provide essential testimony into a coal-mining-union corruption caper. One of the first issues I had to resolve was what local law enforcement, if any, could be involved in her detail. It was always important to involve locals if you could trust them. There were now numerous people in the program, and we were stretched thin. Ultimately, following a security clearance, her detail would consist of four security people: two state policemen, one deputy sheriff, and one matron. A total of twenty-two matrons—women who, while not in the ranks of law enforcement, were nonetheless specially trained to deal with prisoners—were used during the rotation. All except the matrons would live on-site twenty-four hours a day. I authorized payment in the amount of $7,730.60 for two months of meals and lodging. The detail lived in a condo that we rented, and meals were signed for at the main lodge at Silver Springs, a resort area in Fayette County, Pennsylvania.

At the initial contact I had with her, I read her the rules of her protection, and she seemed very alert. She was average looking, rather tall at five foot seven, and weighed about 140 pounds. Her most noticeable feature, however, was her cold eyes. At first I thought she was shy and very protective of her four-year-old son. I was right about the latter but dead wrong about the former. I eventually learned that it was *her* idea to shoot the Yablonskis. The original plan was to blow up the house, but she wanted to make sure they were actually dead, so she changed the plan to a close-up kill.

The Yablonski murders were discovered on January 5, 1970. It was Inauguration Day for state officeholders in Pennsylvania.

Jock Yablonski was prominent on the political scene, so his absence from the swearing-in ceremony was conspicuous. His son, noting the absence, drove to the family farmhouse in Clarksville. In chilling testimony, he stated that he first found the mother in the master bedroom but barely recognized her because her face was stained dark as caked blood covered her face from the two bullet wounds in her head. He then frantically searched for his father. Since his father sometimes snored, he would on occasion sleep in another room. Off the son went to see if his father was alive. En route to another bedroom, he next discovered his sister lying face down on a bed with the quilt soaked in blood. Unable to find his father, he returned to his parents' bedroom. He then saw his father next to the bed in a kneeling position, propped up against an end table. Jock had five shells pumped into him; his wife and their daughter had two apiece.

At trial, the motive for the murders became clear: the Yablonski family was eliminated because of the challenge Jock represented to the reelection of the incumbent, Tony Boyle, in an upcoming vote for top spot in the United Mine Workers of America. Yablonski, urged on by consumer advocate Ralph Nader, who bemoaned the lack of safety for mineworkers, also announced his candidacy for the presidency of the union. That fateful decision marked him for the hit that was carried out by Gilly and company.

Tony Boyle was indicted in March 1971 for misuse of union funds and illegal campaign contributions. That investigation also uncovered $20,000 that was paid to the assassins, which resulted in the murder charge. In April 1974, Boyle was also convicted for the Yablonski murders and sentenced to life in prison. He died behind bars in 1985.

Annette Gilly had to be kept alive to testify against the others involved in union corruption. The Witness Protection

Program at this point was admitting other witnesses to crime besides those perpetrated by the mob. This forced me to use local law enforcement and her case was the first large scale use of this collaboration.

The Annette Gilly detail using the locals was hardly a resounding success. Annette Gilly and her reason for being there became known to all the resort employees. And instead of leaving some guards back at home base, all moves at all times were made by the entire group, which left a lot to be desired of the security situation. A bomb infiltration into the apartment would have been relatively easy while the detail was journeying together.

The detail also kept all equipment in the trunk of the assigned vehicle—one L1 police radio, four shotguns, one Thompson machine gun, and two flak jackets. It would have been difficult to reach the ammo in the event of an attack.

I was lucky nothing had happened to Gilly by the time I caught up with the security lapses. I relocated her to an A-frame house at the end of a dead-end road. The house was at a high level overlooking the entire area. Again, all personnel would live there, and meals were to be cooked on site. I ordered better prisoner control; Gilly had been outside twice a day, and I changed the rule to only once a week. I wasn't happy that she was in coal-mining territory either, but it was a trade-off between that and traveling long distances. I was happy when her testimony was concluded. She received a new ID and moved on with her life.

15

UNCLE SAM, CAN YOU SPARE A DIME?

Sometimes I wonder how otherwise upstanding individuals get themselves in a jam with the wise guys. For instance, Sanford E. Rafsky grew up in Queens, New York, with a family whose income was above average. He was married with an adoring wife and three kids, all of whom turned out well. His seven-room home in Rego Park was a luxury apartment. Both he and his wife had been active in the community for years. He involved himself in the Forest Hills Little League and the Forest Hills Pop Warner League. Citations papered his walls at home, along with awards and plaques attesting to the fact that he was a member of the New York Society of Professional Engineers and the American Association of Industrial Engineers. Framed sheepskins confirmed his consultancy with the Organization of American States, the America Bar Association, the Missouri Bar Association (on economics). These encircled his Bachelor of Science degree in industrial engineering from Penn State. On the desk in his study were notebooks crammed with over one hundred articles he had written.

Rafsky's wife sure didn't understand how her spouse had fallen so badly. He was an avid practitioner of his Jewish faith in the Conservative tradition. For that matter she didn't understand how his father, who was trained to be a rabbi, had come to be charged with mail fraud with Sanford earlier in their careers. She felt certain that Sanford had gotten past that first brush with the law, yet he was on the brink of pleading guilty to defrauding the United States Small Business Administration (SBA). His one year in the graduate program of the University of Pennsylvania's Wharton Business School and his two years at New York University Law School went for naught as he sank deeper and deeper into the hole.

Rafsky and three of his partners had cooked up a scheme to secure $350,000 in loans for each of four dummy corporations. Fabricated financial statements were submitted to the local branch of the SBA in Richmond, Virginia. Rafsky was the chief organizer, promoter, and financial consultant of all of these four corporations. In the pipeline were falsified documents that could have delivered a potential loss to the government in excess of $11,000,000 had Uncle Sam not caught on. All the corporate presidents were charged, along with the head of the Richmond SBA, who had received kickbacks.

The FBI thought it had hit pay dirt when the corrupt government official was implicated. But then Rafsky came clean with a story that sounded like it was from a movie about the mob. It seems that he and his partners, Alexander Heller, Howard Horowitz, and Herbert Zucker (the latter two also implicated in the SBA loan fraud), were motivated in part by the fact that they owed beaucoup bucks to loan sharks. The four men had been owners of Z and H, Inc., a Florida ladies' sports clothes company. The company name came from the partners' initials but excluded Rafsky's because he had gone bankrupt personally recently.

Thinking that the best of times were ahead of them in their new business, the four of them had taken a fateful trip to the Aladdin Hotel in Las Vegas and secured $35,000 in credit. They gambled briefly, losing about $3200, cashed in their chips, and returned home, stiffing the hotel some $32,000 without paying the credit line of $35,000. Shortly thereafter, two burly guys arrived at their plant and threatened them with physical harm unless they paid their debt to the hotel. They gave $5000 to the men to give to Chink Facchiano, who apparently had enough drag to rub Aladdin's lamp and make the debt disappear. Perhaps this made the businessmen too cocky.

By mid-1973 Z&H couldn't pay its bills, so Rafsky and company borrowed money from two different loan sharks. Chink made two extortionate loans, and three came from Francis Jigger Santo. Thus the vicious cycle began. Unable to pay the juice on the loans, they turned to other loan sharks. One guy offered to loan them $10,000 with a 3 percent interest per week or 156 percent annual interest. They turned that offer down but soon accepted two other loans at 2 percent per week and 1.5 percent per week. The partners had ten weeks to pay, but business was still bad. So they began to rob Peter to pay Paul with the SBA ruse. The partners had been warned not to mess up the payback, or else they'd have some missing body parts. Apparently, they thought that Uncle Sam wouldn't hack off a finger, so they set out to stiff the government.

Still reeling from a bad business climate, the partners borrowed money again and again at the same exorbitant rates. The loans grew from $10,000 to $20,000 when Rafsky got the bright idea to solve their financial problems by purchasing two race horses, Jigger's Gal (a nice touch for the loan shark) and Sew for Four. Cash-flow problems remained unabated, and the men continued to borrow more and more money. The SBA scheme escalated as the loan sharks started charging 3 percent per week. Around this time the SBA cut off the spigot. Rafsky and his guys still owed big-time on the newest loans. Emissaries were sent by the loan sharks to tell the business partners that they were going to have their legs broken. The hoods from Santo's operation offered to take the racehorses in lieu of payment. Rafsky tried to buy more time. The final warning was that Rafsky would have his legs broken, his wife and children would be kidnapped, and the horses would be shot or have their legs broken unless payment was forthcoming within twenty-four hours.

Sanford Rafsky decided to sing to get his family into witness protection. This tale brought him to my care and would result in a dragnet of the biggest loan sharks in Florida.

The first time I met Rafsky, I thought he looked like a frail scholar. He was five feet eight inches tall and weighed around 145 pounds with blue eyes and dark-brown hair. I tried not to focus on a one-and-a-quarter-inch depression on the front left part of his skull, but he saw me glance at it and explained that the dent was the result of a fracture as a child. He went on to volunteer that he had also been hit by a horseshoe at a beach game and had been incapacitated for five months. My friend Dr. Robert Farrelly had examined Rafsky's medical records and informed me that he had osteomyelitis, an inflammatory disease of the bone that introduces an infection into the blood tissues and bone marrow. He was limited to nonstrenuous activity and was occasionally subject to fainting spells. When he was relocated, his medical management was going to be a huge issue.

After introducing myself to Rafsky, I soon learned why this guy could con a dog into giving up a bone. With his above-average intelligence and charm, he was a smooth and persuasive conversationalist. He struck me as having a genuine concern for the safety of his family. Arrangements were made to harbor them and give them a change of identity, although it took much longer than it should have done because at that time I had to ask Washington to agree to all arrangements. Rafsky received a prison sentence but was assigned to prisons where the risk to his safety was minimal. He was to receive financial assistance for six months upon release.

I was with him when he had to be returned to the zone of danger. The Feds needed to debrief him. We had placed him in a prison in New Hampshire, so I had to pick him up there and transport him to Florida to go through boxes of documents for the SBA case as well as the loan-sharking trial. We stayed outside prison because they weren't safe places and I didn't want to risk his life.

Another time I had to take him to New York then back again to New Hampshire. On the day I was to return him to his New Hampshire prison, he had teeth problems and needed work done to save all of his bottom teeth. The facility in New Hampshire wasn't able to perform the dental work, so I asked the dentist to outline what had to be done as well as the seriousness of having it done forthwith. But because the Justice Department was so slow to authorize the work, it took close to a month to fix the problem. The guy had drains in his mouth for days. I never did get him back to the New Hampshire jail, even though we were in New Hampshire at the dentist, because I had to transport him to New York to appear before a grand jury. Three weeks later, we were headed to the federal court in Richmond, Virginia, where the SBA plot was explained to a grand jury.

While all this was going on, Rafsky was seething over the fact that Washington hadn't signed his Memorandum of Understanding, the contract of mutual rights and responsibilities between him and the Justice Department. I thought this was chicken dung by the Assistant Chief of Security who had interposed another layer of bureaucracy for more Justice folks to sign off on the plan. I thought it was nothing but a "cover one's butt" practice. The delays caused unnecessary tension. It wasn't a great performance by my department, particularly given that the guy also almost lost his bottom choppers. He was one guy whose beefs had merit.

As for the loan sharking case, the defendants were convicted and found themselves on the receiving end of double digit jail sentences since they were charged under the Racketeer Influenced and Corrupt Organizations (RICO) Act. Their respective appeals were rebuffed by the Eleventh Circuit. Rafsky got the last laugh. Eventually he was paroled, and I got him a new name through a probate court proceeding. I haven't heard from him since.

16

PRINCE OF THE CITY

W here the hell are you from—Arizona?" Bob Leuci asked, staring at my cowboy boots.

We were in the Southern District of New York, the office of then assistant U.S. attorney Rudy Giuliani. Giuliani had asked me to place Leuci in the Witness Protection Program, but Bob wasn't buying it.

Robert Leuci was a gung-ho rookie New York City police officer in 1961. His first assignment was at the 100th Precinct in Rockaway Beach, Queens. Later, he became a member of the tactical patrol force of the New York Police Department (NYPD). He had worked the most active of the city's precincts, amassing an impressive record of arrests. He looked very young in those days and had picked up the nickname Babyface. Because of his record of arrests and the fact that he didn't look at all like a cop, he was offered an assignment in the public morals unit, an assignment he had turned down because Public Morals had a long and dark history of institutionalized corruption that went back to the time of Prohibition. Enforcing the gambling, prostitution, and all sorts of public morals laws, Plainclothes, as it was called, was a moneymaking machine. It was not a place for a young and idealistic cop.

The narcotics division, on the other hand, had a reputation

for being clean, and so that's where Babyface wanted to work three years after joining the force. As subsequent events would unfold, he'd find out that the reputation was undeserved.

After only three years in uniform with the Narcotics Division, Leuci was promoted to the Detective Bureau of this unit. His first job was to infiltrate East New York Vocational High School as a student and buy drugs.

These were the wild, free-love, drug-crazed days of the mid-sixties. Our country was in the midst of enormous struggles: war in Vietnam and civil unrest at home. Immense changes were taking place. A heroin epidemic was sweeping the land, especially in New York, and hordes of addicts ran in the streets. Civil unrest, drugs, money, and rock and roll were the fashions of the times. People played by their own rules, a downward spiral affecting all the elements of society. Immorality was carried on the wings of social disruption and metastasized throughout society—and the Narcotics Bureau of the NYPD was not immune.

The NYPD's narcotics division became totally corrupt. Everyone was touched by it, including Leuci. He was slipped $500 by two other cops in the division for his share of a gambling payoff. He gave half to his sergeant, playing by the rules of the internal payoff system among crooked cops. With that, his peers summarily accepted him. Now he was asked to join them for drinks after work and barbecues at the weekends; overnight he had become a stand-up guy. But Leuci set his own rules. When he was the lead partner, he told his junior officer that if money was hanging around in a drug bust, he'd skim some off the top and share it, but he drew the line at shaking somebody down or accepting a bribe to let a drug dealer go.

Enter the Knapp Commission formed in 1970. In 1971 the Knapp Commission was listening to police officer Frank Serpico and others about the extent of corruption that had come to permeate the entire New York City police force. Mistakenly, Leuci's name was dropped as the only honest cop in Narcotics. Soon commission counsel Nick Scoppetta was importuning Leuci to cooperate with the commission. Leuci was adamant that he wouldn't investigate cops, but little by little he became involved in an investigation covering the entire New York City criminal justice system. He was undercover for sixteen months. This was beyond the scope of the Knapp Commission, so Scoppetta went to the federal government for financing of a probe. Scoppetta and the Feds began a long-term, deep-cover investigation into corruption throughout the criminal justice system in New York City. Judges, bail bondsmen, prosecutors, defense lawyers, and organized-crime figures were the targets, and Leuci was the lead undercover agent.

Deep undercover cases are complicated, and eventually Leuci did what he had sworn he'd never do: he wore a wire to record fellow officers as they implicated themselves in wrongdoing.

Leuci became an enemy of the mob and drug dealers on one side and corrupt justice system participants on the other. Giuliani wanted to ensure that Leuci lived to make the cases, and so I was invited to meet the five feet ten inch cop who was built like a boxer. He was just as combative as a boxer, too. Leuci stared right at me: "I'm not going into the Witness Protection Program. Only bad guys do that. I'm not a fucking criminal. I'm a detective, not under arrest or threatened with arrest, I'm doing this case voluntarily. I'm not gonna look like a crook."

Rudy Giuliani tried to reason with him. "You've got a wife and two toddlers, age two and five. You've got to make decisions to move them out of harm's way."

Back and forth they argued. Just when I thought he was convinced, Leuci looked at me with scorn: "I don't want federal marshals guarding me."

"We're the only people who can save your sorry ass," I responded.

"Look, I've heard of you, Partington. I'm not insulting you. It's just that if I'm going to be protected, I want my own guys around."

Leuci wanted motorcycle cops—three of them, one for each eight-hour shift—because they drove well. He would handpick three other cops from tough precincts, because they were capable in the street and he had known one of them since childhood, when they played in a sandbox together. He wanted three mounted police, because if they had to testify, they'd look great on the stand and add credibility to his testimony—mounted cops were the best-dressed and best-looking cops on the job. When he went to court, they would be with him. One cop from each group would serve three rotating shifts.

Eventually we came up with a compromise. The New York police whom we vetted would guard Leuci Monday through Friday. During the week, marshals would guard his wife and children, on the weekends the city cops would deliver Bob, and marshals would guard him and the family around the clock.

Somewhat mollified, Leuci began to tell me why he was so insistent about the cops and how and why he had become involved in the investigation.

I shut him off. "Look, if you are Rudy's guy, you're my guy. I don't need or want any explanations. You're a brother."

Rudy Giuliani started to ask me about the new names for the Leuci family.

"I'm not using any name but my own," Leuci said. "Nor is my family." He had it in his head that to change his name would make him look like the bad guys in the Witness Protection Program. I thought the point wasn't worth fighting about. His children were too young for school, and his wife, Gina, would never be out of the marshals' sight.

Leuci wanted to make sure that I understood that he was still a cop. He'd be reporting every day to Giuliani's office. He'd keep his gun. He had bargained with the commissioner of police that his work would count toward his pension. He'd been on the job for fifteen years by the time I met him. He needed five more years to earn his retirement and pension, so he was "on assignment" to the prosecutor's office. I didn't care one way or another about any deal he had made. My job was to keep him alive.

Rudy Giuliani had informed both Leuci and me that the FBI in Las Vegas had picked up information that he was to be killed by an assassin for $3,000. Bob Leuci was insulted by the low amount.

Prior to my meeting him, Detective Leuci had worn a wire on 110 occasions, had risked death, and had given Giuliani's office an astounding amount of evidence against an array of people both within and outside the justice system. New York was an open city for the right price. The charges were about to be announced, so it was my task to whisk Leuci away to safety and ensure his return each day to the U.S. Attorney's Office for case preparation.

Finally we were ready to go. I took Leuci downstairs into the indoor parking garage. Two tall marshals held carbines. I got into the lead car with Leuci, and three cars followed behind.

I made sure that nobody else would be on the ferry to Governors Island, where we would house Leuci in a Coast Guard facility. Upon arriving at the island, Leuci seemed impressed by the grid of protection I had set up. A show of force was necessary to deter any wannabe hit men. Meanwhile, a contingent of nine marshals accompanied his family to the family's cabin in the Catskills.

I made a point of using only marshals who were "country boys," as opposed to New York–based marshals. Since this investigation could reach the highest echelons, and some marshals were ex-cops, I wanted to make sure I avoided the who-knows-whom problem. Besides, it was wintertime, and I needed robust marshals to police the Catskill Mountains, which were mighty cold in winter.

After about four weeks, Bob Leuci was going stir-crazy not seeing his family. I was off setting up other witnesses' safe houses when I got a call from assistant D.A. Elliot Sager and Bob Morvillo, who later made a name for himself as Martha Stewart's attorney.

"This guy asked me to call you," Sager said. "He just knocked over a desk. He's refusing to work and prepare cases unless we let him see his family. I told the asshole that all the roads are blocked. We have a fuckin' blizzard here."

"Bring him to the heliport on Wall Street," I directed. I knew a helicopter pilot, Mickey Tobin, a former Vietnam pilot, who worked for Customs. We arrived at the Wall Street heliport at around 5 P.M. I loved the expression on Leuci's face when he spotted Tobin, who looked about twelve.

"Hey Mickey," Leuci said, "how've you been?" I was astounded. Mickey and Leuci had worked the Special Investigations Unit of the Narcotics Division together. Leuci knew Mickey, but that didn't deter him from hopping into the helicopter.

Mickey Tobin gave us the ride of our lives. We went under the 59th Street Bridge and under the Tappan Zee Bridge. Leuci loved it. I could see why he made a great street cop—he loved danger.

"So where are we goin'?" Tobin asked.

"What?" Leuci said. "You don't know?"

After Leuci told him the site, Tobin studied the map, wondering how we were going to see where to land. I had phoned ahead and directed the marshals to circle a field near the house.

I told them to keep their automobiles' headlights on. We finally spotted the circle after a few tense moments. Mickey then announced that because of the snow he was having a depth-perception problem, so he'd have to get as close as he thought he could, and we'd have to jump. Bob let out a spew of expletives that might have sounded like a prayer except for his tone of voice.

"This is it, boys," Tobin directed.

Still praying, Leuci went first and I went second. Fortunately, we were only four feet above the ground. On the way to the house, we laughed like crazy about our trip. The ice was broken between us, but that didn't mean that guarding him was a bed of roses.

One marshal I appointed to guard him stayed out and guarded the house from high up in a tree. Bob's wife was used to cooking for all the guards, and they were rotated inside the house to warm up, but this marshal refused to come in out of the cold and brought his own rations. Bob complained that the guy was strange. "No," I said. "He's just different."

There was one really strange marshal assigned to guard Leuci. He was handsome, blond, and built like a six-foot brick. One night Leuci got a call from the New Jersey police. "We've got a guy here who says his job is guarding you." The cops had picked him up. He was found naked with a girl in a car. He'd also been drinking and had several guns in the car.

Bob went to get him out of jail, and I had a decision to make. Ordinarily, I would have fired the guy, but Bob liked and trusted him. He'd had a bad time in Vietnam. He'd come home injured—not physically, but there were holes in his mind that booze and thrills filled up. He promised he'd straighten himself out, and Leuci spoke up for him. I decided to give him another chance. That was a mistake. Sometime later, he fell off the edge. It happens. He kidnapped the wife of a Mafia guy—he thought he was in love with her. There were stories that he was sleeping with jurors, that he was a ladies' man and totally warped, another casualty of the Vietnam War. I finally canned him.

I'd often meet with Leuci to see how he was doing. We'd exchange cop stories. He had an interesting perspective on the cops' so-called blue wall of silence: "You hate the drug dealers and their lawyers. They're always ready to expound on police brutality or corruption. Yet I never met a defense lawyer who regularly defends the dope guys who didn't offer me something dirty to have the charges go away or be reduced. And I gotta listen to them pontificate about police corruption?"

He added to the list of those he held in contempt: "Prosecutors were no bargain either. Judges, bail bondsmen, *everyone* in the New York criminal justice system was touched by corruption, but all anyone seems to focus on is the police. It's bullshit."

During some of our conversations I really believed that Bob thought he wouldn't have to turn in his fellow cops because of the bigger fish he'd made helped the Feds catch. He was wrong. Some of these cops invited themselves into the action while Bob was wearing a wire. He seemed genuinely pained when he had to testify against them.

In all, Bob made about fifty cases, many with multiple defendants. Marshals transported him to ten cases in which he had to testify; the others were all pleas. The once-elite Special Investigations Unit of the Narcotics Division, was decimated by corruption probes. Of approximately seventy men who were known as the "Princes of the City" because of their elite status, some fifty-two were indicted. Others were fired.

A major cases that was axiomatic of the type of prosecutions was that of a defense lawyer named Edmund Rosner. Rosner, along with a bail bondsman and a corrupt detective, tried to buy secret, federal grand jury testimony. All three were convicted.

Alan Dershowitz unsuccessfully argued the appeal by impugning Leuci. The convictions stood.

Things really tightened up for Leuci when the police department discovered that almost all of the major drugs seized in New York City had been stolen from the clerk's office. Tom Puccio, U.S. attorney in the Eastern District (who would later gain notoriety as the legal counsel for Claus von Bülow), headed up the investigation.[1] Between 1969 and 1972, 398 pounds of heroin and cocaine had been stolen, and Puccio was going to find out who did it. Much of the stolen heroin had been seized in 1962 as a result of the celebrated French Connection case.

Puccio believed that Leuci might not have been involved, but his bet was that Leuci would know who was. The investigation stayed inactive until assistant D.A. Puccio decided to make a "connection" with Leuci.

The former Prince of the City was about to be uncrowned.

---

1. Claus on Bülow was on trial in Rhode Island for the attempted murder of his wife, Sunny von Bülow. In his first trial, he was found guilty. The Rhode Island Supreme Court reversed the conviction on technical grounds and ordered a new trial. In 1985 von Bülow was retried, represented by Tom Puccio and prosecuted under this author's office as Attorney General, and was acquitted.

17

BLOODY BUT UNBOWED

I feel like I have a tiger on my back that I can't shake off," said Bob Leuci, pacing the room like a big caged cat himself. The many months of testifying against corrupt prosecutors, judges, bondsmen, and, alas, cops, had caught up to him. As implausible as it seemed, life had just gotten worse.

"Can you believe this asshole?" Leuci muttered. He was referring to Tom Puccio, chief of the Criminal Division of the Eastern District of New York. Puccio was investigating the theft of the entire cache of drugs that was seized during the French Connection.

The French Connection case had become a legend because it was a great grab of dope—and because it was memorialized in the movie of the same name. Gene Hackman and Roy Scheider played the two daring New York cops whose 1962 heroin bust was the largest in New York history. In addition to winning Best Picture at the Oscars in 1971, the movie scored four other Oscars. The movie made the high-profile case even more visible. Losing the drugs was mighty embarrassing for law enforcement.

After the original bust, the heroin, stored in fourteen large plastic bags in a blue suitcase and two red suitcases that were themselves placed in a large, black steamer trunk, was vouchered by the NYPD Property Clerk Division at 400 Broome

Street. The Broome Street building had been a former candy factory uncharacteristically built with iron doors and walls that were eight feet thick. Drugs were supposedly kept in a safe area in the building. The Property Clerk Division was responsible for the care of all evidence from crimes.

While impenetrable on the outside, the Property Office was subject to incursion from the inside. On court days, New York's Finest would queue up outside the property clerk's evidence window. The officer could sign out evidence by name and badge number. Obviously, there were so many cops that the clerk didn't necessarily know the officer by sight, and unlike today, there were no picture IDs.

The French Connection drugs were signed out several times. The load went before a grand jury; at other times it was present at the court proceedings against the defendants. Prosecutors could have used only a tiny portion of the drugs once they were tested and had the rest destroyed, but as part of a trial tactic they liked to bring in the huge stash to show the jury just how much the bad guys were poisoning people through the sale of illegal narcotics. Politics also had a hand in this dog and pony show. A year after the seizure, the heroin was checked out of the property office and driven to Washington, D.C., where it was displayed before a U.S. Senate committee studying heroin trafficking. Despite a street value at that time of more than $30 million, it was shipped back to New York by the Railway Express Agency without escort. It was placed back in its "safe area," where containers of other drugs like marijuana had been eaten through by mice and drugs often spilled out of their respective containers onto the floor.

After the conclusion of the trial, the drugs remained in the property room, probably because the police were still trying literally to make the French Connection since the European counterparts were never captured (and still haven't been, despite a sequel to the movie which implied that they had been caught). For five years the drugs lay in obscurity, guarded by spiders.

The New York police did not know the drugs had been pilfered until a young NYPD detective named James (J.J.) Farley rang a doorbell in a suburban house in Nassau County.[1] He'd say that he was an Allstate Insurance guy and would get himself invited in by his female prey, whom he'd rape once inside the house. This time, though, the police were ready with a decoy and arrested him. His house was later searched pursuant to a warrant, and the officers found brown manila envelopes from the property clerk's office filled with drugs. Farley, who had about a dozen rape cases filed against him, was unfazed by this infraction; he launched into an explanation that exposed the holes in the voucher system. This led to the audit of the narcotics section on Broome Street.

The last itemized handling of the French Connection drugs was on September 29, 1969. A Detective Nuzziato, detective shield 3495, had signed out the dope. It was never signed back in. When the auditors examined the area where the drugs were supposed to be and brought the contents to the police chemists' lab, the "drugs" were crawling with flour beetles. Flour beetles die on heroin. These buggers were so fat they were doing push-ups. Nearly four hundred pounds of heroin had disappeared.

There was no Detective Nuzziato in the city's police department. The closest name was that of Detective Joe Nunziata, but the badge number didn't match his. Nunziata was part of the same elite drug-busting unit as Leuci. In fact, he was Leuci's partner. Hence Tom Puccio was going to squeeze Leuci in order to crack the case.

Puccio suspected that Nunziata had been at least a party to the theft. He was a smart guy—so smart, in fact, that he might

---

1. Gregory Wallance, *Papa's Game* (Rawson, Wade Publishers, 1981).

"implicate" himself with a misspelled name and wrong badge number. His defense would be that it was a setup because he knew how to write his name and badge number.

Leuci was steaming: "Puccio and his investigators had me write out Joe Nunziata's name a half dozen times. I felt like a schoolkid writing badge numbers. That dumb shit Puccio thinks I'm involved." Bob later calmed down when he learned that many of the elite members of the narcotics squad were asked to do the same thing.

For months Bob Leuci was put through the mill. Sometimes Puccio would have him sit for hours outside his door and then tell him to go home. One day he brought a foreigner into the office while Leuci was there. The guy, who was later described as a drug dealer whom Leuci had arrested, spat on the floor and exited.

"What's that all about?" Leuci asked Puccio.

"He says you shook him down for $400. He gave it to you and you still arrested him."

I can just imagine how ballistic this accusation made Leuci. He had smoke coming out of his ears as he recounted the accusation.

"I'm no fuckin' altar boy, John, but I never let dope dealers off. I'd skim money from the off top of a drug bust, but I never took money in exchange for anything, let alone freedom for a drug peddler." As the conversation wore on, Leuci became even more livid that Puccio would think that he'd do such a stupid thing. "Never, never," he ranted. "And that shit thinks I'd do a thing like that for $400?"

"Calm down, brother," I counseled. I thought Puccio's tactics were working, because he had Leuci on the defensive.

One by one, detectives were brought in from Leuci's former unit. Puccio was planning on indicting them on other drug-related graft. The game was that in exchange for a lesser plea, the detectives would drop the dime on Leuci and his partner, Nunziata, as the brain trust behind the theft of the French Connection drugs. He'd be the easy guy to blame, since the cops hated him for his undercover corruption work.

While I was handling other witnesses, I made a point to try to interact as much as possible with Leuci. I didn't want him to think that all of us in law enforcement despised him.

Weeks turned into months, and the drilling of Bob Leuci continued unabated. Sometimes he wouldn't return to our safe house until he'd been at Puccio's office for twelve or fourteen hours. Then came a devastating blow: Leuci's former partner, Joe Nunziata, ate his gun rather than face the accusations. Another detective, Dave Cody, followed suit. Leuci was beside himself.

My job was to keep my witnesses in a good frame of mind. Leuci was perhaps my biggest challenge. It was clear he had loved being a cop. He upbraided himself for participating in the corruption. Now he was reeling from the suicides of two guys with whom he had been close.

Leuci certainly didn't get much time to mourn. The suicides were flung in Leuci's face as evidence that they must have been in on the robbery of the drugs, so Leuci must be guilty, too. Leuci was at the same time being debriefed about new corruption cases he was making, preparing for his testimony on cases he had already scored, and yet being subjected to an inquisition in-between times where he didn't know whether he'd be arrested based on somebody's payback.

"I'm going to take a lie-detector test, John, so these fuckers will know that I have nothing to do with the French Connection. I'll do sodium pentothal, hypnotism, truth serum, whatever they want." I told him to think hard about doing this, since he was a nervous wreck and that could affect the test.

Puccio continued to bang Leuci about being indicted now for

the alleged $400 kickback from the drug dealer he'd brought into the office. "John, that Puccio could indict the Gingerbread Man if he had a mind to," Leuci told me. At one point, Puccio told Leuci that he better come back with the names of the culprits for the French Connection caper by 5 P.M. Leuci called me, outraged by the proposal: "Fuck five o'clock," he said and hung up.

Five P.M. came and went. No indictment.

Puccio kept this mind game up with Bob for a long time. Perhaps that's being a good prosecutor. It certainly wreaked havoc with Bob, but the evidence never led back to him. Frank King, an investigator, a couple of cops, and Vincent Papa, a major drug dealer, got tagged with the crime but were never successfully prosecuted for the theft. King, for example, was convicted in a tax-evasion case. Papa went to the federal Atlanta Federal Penitentiary, a high-rise zoo, the same one Raymond Patriarca was in, for selling drugs.

The French Connection case resurfaced again in 2009. Anthony Casso, one of the most feared underbosses of the Lucchese family, was serving life sentences totaling 455 years for murders. He constantly wrote to law enforcement seeking "sunlight" in exchange for details on other murders and for fingering who took the infamous dope from the police vault. He claimed that four narcotic detectives scooped the heroin. One worked inside the property clerk's office, one was later shot to death, and he could finger the other two, he wrote to NYPD detective Pat Alteiri. He could even find the gun that killed the cop if he could get a ride around New York. As he's an escape risk, it's doubtful that law enforcement officials will ever take the bait. Besides, it would take a ton of corroboration to confirm his version of the story. Officials seemed content to let him stew in one of the highest-security jails for his fifteen murders and ties to twenty-two others.

I tried never to get personal with any of the folks that I protected. I really only needed to know events in their past that might target them for assassination. I must say, however, that despite his past failings, Leuci had guts. Frank Serpico, another cop who helped the Knapp Commission clean up crime in the New York Police Department, never had to actually testify. Bob Leuci had to put his life and reputation on the line at every level to uncover the justice-for-sale scheme in New York. Today Leuci's an acclaimed author. I was glad to see Babyface Leuci make it.

18

COP WANNABE

One of the guys I ended up protecting was a young hood by the name of Vinny Ensulo, one of Bob Leuci's informants. He had quite an introduction to Leuci when Leuci patrolled the streets. As a newly minted detective, Bob Leuci's beat was Brooklyn. One night he and his partner were riding around and spotted a hooker who had been injured. A man the size of a beefeater had roughed her up and taken money from her.

The description of the perp was a guy wearing a red sweatshirt with a hood, so Leuci started after Red Riding Hood. Other streetwalkers had also reported to Leuci that they'd been ripped off by the same guy. Eventually, the patrolmen spotted him, and all five feet ten inches of Leuci got out of the car to confront the six foot six inch Ensulo, whose biceps were bigger than Leuci's head.

"Assume the position," Leuci ordered. Ensulo laughed at him. "Make me." Leuci ordered him again, but to no avail. Leuci spun him around to cuff him. The giant was about to swat Leuci like a fly off his back, when Leuci's partner jammed a gun in Ensulo's neck. "My partner said turn around and put your hands on the wall. Do it!" The gorilla sighed and turned around. They searched him, but there was nothing in his pockets. Leuci warned him that if he hurt another woman on the streets he'd find him and plant ten bags of dope in his pocket. As Leuci told me, he was lecturing the guy when a car came forward carrying a gangster named Nicky Conforti. The window was rolled down, and out came a hand with a pistol pointed toward the trio. Leuci screamed to everybody to get down. Ensulo, however, screamed like a banshee and took after the car. Hurling a soda bottle at the departing vehicle, Ensulo chased the car until it was out of sight. Thus began the relationship between Ensulo, a onetime prizefighter, and Leuci.

For some reason Ensulo liked Leuci. Ensulo was robbing others to support a drug habit. He thought that he was the lion and the king of the street jungle. Eventually he offered to be an informant, and Leuci would pay him by subtracting some cocaine from a bust and giving it to him. His real contribution was to turn in house dealers. Because of the laws governing search and seizures of homes and apartments, it was very difficult to make a case against house dealers. Street dealers were easy prey since they were conducting business out in the open. Ensulo's tips became the key to unlocking the doors of dealers behind doors.

Vinny Ensulo ran a tile and rug business in Brooklyn. On November 1, 1973, he was in an automobile with James Gallo and Joseph Conigliaro, two major drug lords. Ensulo was sitting in the middle. Gallo and Conigliaro took out their guns and fired them at Ensulo to bump him off. Instead they shot each other in the scuffle and merely wounded Ensulo. This ill-fated ride brought him to our door, since he was to testify against these guys.

When I met Vinny Ensulo I thought he looked like an Italian Refrigerator Perry, the Chicago Bears football player. He seemed to fancy himself as part of the law enforcement team. He didn't act like somebody in protected custody. He was forever asking to attend briefings. In fact, he got a little bored between testifying so he started to turn in other criminals, particularly in the loan-sharking business.

After he had successfully testified in 1973 against loan sharks and against drug-dealers Gallo and Conigliaro, I relocated him to Federal Hill in Providence under the name Vincent Ennis. He opened a flower shop, but he just couldn't adjust. I'd thought that Federal Hill, an ethnic Italian neighborhood, would be perfect for him, but he missed Brooklyn. Against my advice, he moved back home.

On April 14, 1978, Ensulo was working as a cabdriver. He was shot to death that morning as he stepped out of a coffee shop he frequented at 57th Street and Eleventh Avenue in Manhattan. One lesson, which we preached to protected witnesses, was to avoid any routine. Vinny Ensulo had apparently ignored the admonition; he was plugged four times in the back. I felt badly.

Shortly after his murder, the car carrying the assailants was found ablaze under the West Side Highway. It had been stolen. To my knowledge nobody was convicted of Ensulo's murder, although the suspects were the recently released Gallo and Conigliaro. A telling talisman was found in Ensulo's cab. Police reported finding two miniature badges resembling police or other law enforcement insignia. In his own way he was part of a law enforcement family.

19

SPLITTING AT THE SEAMS

By 1980 the Witness Protection Program was packing in more witnesses than it could handle. When I first set it up, at most seventy-five witnesses plus their families were absorbed each year. There were few complaints, and not a single witness following the guidelines was murdered. But in the early eighties, roughly five hundred witnesses were being added to the roster annually, which, including families, meant fifteen hundred additional people who needed protection along with the alumni. We didn't have the budget nor the manpower to protect them. To make matters worse, law enforcement and prosecutors were seeing the witnesses before the marshals did and promising them the moon and the stars. These promises would be broken. It wasn't fair to the prospective witness to come into the program under false pretenses. Additionally, the public was at risk, because the monitoring of relocated participants was minimal due to strained resources.

With the influx of witnesses and families, horror stories of murder and mayhem soon became public. The Witness Protection Program, originally envisioned to go after the Mafia had been extended to protect witnesses who would testify against the Russian and Chinese mobs. This was laudable in that La Cosa Nostra, a.k.a. the Mafia, was being dismantled as a result of myriad prosecutions due to the program, but the resources weren't made available for the incorporation of the Russians and Chinese nor for the unique cultural issues inherent in their absorption.

Some witnesses were now coming into the program who were not of the caliber of earlier witnesses; they should never have been awarded protected status, given the lightweight information they were able to provide. Taking a chapter from the success of the mob witnesses, prosecutors started to pack drug-caper witnesses into the program. Soon, 50 percent of entrants were on narcotics-related cases. One, Warren Simms, was placed in the program in 1978 after he helped convict some drug dealers. Subsequently, he and his daughter would rob a bank under their new alias. She accidentally shot herself when confronted by the police, and her father shot it out with the cops after the robbery. He got a lesser sentence of twenty years because his records were protected (otherwise he would have been tugged with a life sentence had his bodyguard been known). This hardly seemed to be the best utilization of the program.

Some of the deputy marshals lost their way because they, too, weren't screened carefully enough and were sometimes mesmerized by the big money earned by their charges. A San Diego marshal began socializing with a protected witness and even borrowed $10,000 from the witness. The deputy mentioned the name of a business rival, whom the witness promptly offed. Again, hardly the purpose of the Witness Protection Program.

Witnesses who belonged in the program were understandably squawking about being left without proper identification and school records for their kids. The breach of these basics was unconscionable.

Other problems of a more sociological nature emerged. Non-custodial parents were longing for contact with their children.

Usually, the protected witness had been extracted quickly and on an emergency basis, so the divorced or separated parent had no idea where the children were. As bad as this was for the parents, it was worse for the children.

Facilities were becoming overcrowded, and one safe house in Rhode Island was fairly typical of this. For example, during Michael Hellerman's stay in Rhode Island, there were four bedrooms with two to three beds each. There were constant comings and goings, with marshals transporting witnesses to and from debriefings, juries, and trials, not to mention shopping for groceries. Nobody was allowed out at night: a cell-like barred door was locked shut at the top of the staircase leading to the bedrooms, with marshals guarding on that floor and on the staircase.

Recreation was limited—fishing in a back pond, barbells, a pool table, a television (which those on guard duty weren't allowed to watch), chess sets brought in by the marshals, and cards (but no wagering, because I didn't want fights breaking out).

The government allotted only six bucks per witness per day for the safe house. Most of the time the witnesses would pool their money to buy some special food that they could all enjoy. Some guys like Hellerman were pretty good gourmet chefs. Excepting the gourmet nights, the food was pretty basic. Not all the money went into food, though: cigarettes, toiletries, and so on were all to be paid out of the meager allowance.

The house residents had to be up at their appointed time. Some starts were at 5 or 6 A.M. Breakfast, like all meals, had three seatings when the house was crowded. The dinner shifts were hour-long shifts, starting at 6:00 P.M., 7:30 P.M., and 9:00 P.M., respectively.

The witnesses did the house chores; it was somewhat surprising to see these former millionaires doing dishes and washing the pots and pans.

I tried to make sure that the witnesses living together had nothing in common as far as crime was concerned. If somebody were being housed for securities fraud, another would be there for testimony in a narcotics trial, government corruption, or a bank robbery. One of the constant tensions in the house was to make sure that egos stayed in check. While these guys came from different fields, sometimes the conversations among them would deteriorate into a "what I did was tougher than what you did" braggadocio. Another priority was to make sure that we didn't start up minienterprises among the guys. We tried to have peace through diplomacy but we really didn't want any of these people getting close to each other.

It was interesting to learn what bothered these witnesses the most. Hellerman, as mentioned earlier, was deeply troubled that his name would pass without any known progeny. Other witnesses knew that they had to abandon all contact with their mistresses; monogamy was the only way to stay alive. Virtually all of the witnesses missed the limelight. Being a prince, if not a king, was better than being a working stiff. The excitement of the crime was a narcotic. Regular life was boring, although some of my "graduates" managed to take to suburbia after all. Despite having lived through trials, some really worried about future security, which did subsequently become a concern, because the government didn't keep its promises.

In any event, the program wasn't easy street. Danger lurked in reality or in the minds of the participants. I was surprised at how tranquil the marriages were, given the terrible circumstances. Testifying is stressful under normal circumstances. Imagine pointing a finger at a guy who would love nothing better than to put your lights out. I grew to respect the spouses and kids and even the criminal witnesses. It's hard to live with looking over your shoulder for the rest of your life.

As the program began to take in more participants, however,

the groupings began to disappear. More and more witnesses had similar crime backgrounds, so it wasn't wise to lump them together lest they establish their own respective gang once released. Like society outside, the newcomers seemed more stressed. The spartan lifestyle got to them more since they'd been spoiled with so many toys during the time they'd been out on the streets. The program resorted more and more to solitary living situations. Marshal coverage was a constant nagging problem. After the exodus of a family from hands-on protection, we often gave short shrift to their adjustment outside in the world. That's where the problems really began, since we no longer had the kind of contact with the "graduates" that we should have had, for both their adjustments back into society and the safety of the public. Some bad things were about to happen.

20

WHEN WITNESSES WANT MORE

Most informants were gargantuan complainers, sometimes with good cause. Take Herman Goldfarb, whose old life died in October 1974 when his cooperation as an undercover operative in organized crime in New York City's garment district was exposed. He posed as the president of a trucking company set up by the Feds to penetrate racketeering. He was a perfect player for the operation since he had a record and had done jail time for swindling a group of prominent attorneys in an insurance-selling scheme. He could talk a dog off a meat wagon, as the proverbial saying goes. Following thirteen indictments and multiple convictions (three guilty pleas and one conviction following trial) as a result of his testimony, Goldfarb had to dodge a $200,000 contract on his life. That's where I came in. I was responsible for protecting him during the trials and for arranging his transition.

Goldfarb was not an easy mark for cooperation. He was particularly upset that he had to be protected since he generally dismissed the threat to himself and his family. This made him a rather unpleasant guy to deal with—he thought he was bulletproof from any mob hit. After months of negotiation, we agreed to guard him at his home—a deviation from the usual safe-house routine. The U.S. attorney wanted him in the program at any cost.

On the surface, Goldfarb's life looked charmed. He lived in a $100,000 home (in 1977 dollars) and drove a late-model car, all toys from his multi-million-dollar business selling insurance. Apparently, he had negotiated a deal with his Justice Department handlers to keep him in the insurance business, since his license was intact. His chief complaints were that he now lacked privacy because his home was ringed by closed-circuit television cameras and that when he drove to work each morning, he was in constant radio communication with the marshals guarding him. For some reason darkness made him edgy, and his bravado disappeared. He moaned over the fact that he had to be home by 5 P.M. because he was afraid of what might happen to him in the dark. At movies, which he rarely attended, he sat between two members of his family, and as the credits rolled, he waited until the lights went on to leave so he wouldn't be stabbed in the back.

Certainly, his concerns about the hardship on his children adjusting to new schools were legitimate, and he pointed out some real faux pas made by the program. For instance, he and his wife were given social security numbers with digits were precisely a hundred numbers apart, and her birth certificate had a date of birth that made her seem as old as Eve. These mistakes justifiably spooked him.

Goldfarb's other complaints were less valid. He wanted a life insurance policy to protect his family because he had a heart condition. He also wanted a Small Business Administration (SBA) loan when the job was over. He argued that it would be impossible for him to get a job with somebody else, so he had to be his own entrepreneur. But he did not want to invest his own money. He also wanted his prior conviction looked into and possibly expunged, since he said he was innocent even though he had pled guilty.

Benjamin Civiletti, assistant attorney general, nixed the idea of the SBA loan and the insurance policy as being beyond the scope of the program. The Justice Department just couldn't use any special pressure on a bank to give him an SBA-backed loan nor lean on an insurance company to issue a policy if they would otherwise reject him. One excellent insight Civiletti had was to propose that promises were to be made only by marshals, so that they could be monitored and verified. I proposed a written contract outlining precisely what the witness should expect, and Civiletti implemented this suggestion.

Goldfarb did not help his cause. He informed me through his detail that he would not testify unless promises made to him were kept. This position practically guaranteed their denial. At trial the defense would bring up these new incentives and use them to cross-examine his credibility. The demands had to be vetoed. That didn't stop Goldfarb from sending me messages that he was living in a prison without bars. All I could think of was the dump that Joe Barboza had endured for many months on a deserted island, and with far less of the histrionics. Goldfarb also presented his two hundred complaints to Judge Robert Ward of the Federal District Court in Manhattan, who had presided at one of the trials. Civiletti opined that the protection program must be doing something right because there was nothing preventing Goldfarb from leaving the program.

Goldfarb subsequently testified in Project Cleveland, which focused on garment industry infiltration by mobsters. Additionally, he was a witness for the prosecution against mob boss Anthony Pro Provenzano, who had looted the Teamsters pension fund. Goldfarb was present at a meeting—or so he said—which concocted a deal for a $300,000 kickback on a "loan" of two million dollars from union pension funds. Some top wise guys, including Pro, bit the dust as a result of his testimony, although later Goldfarb recanted his testimony against Provenzano.

Although Provenzano was in jail following the trial, his defense team got the conviction overturned because Goldfarb had written a letter to a prosecutor stating that he wasn't sure that the voice asking for the kickback was that of the notorious crime boss. He stated that he wasn't looking directly at Provenzano. This exculpatory info was never turned over to the defense.

Following the trial, there were some accommodations made in light of Goldfarb's complaint list. He and his family got new social security cards and birth certificates, the children's school records were changed, and we provided Goldfarb and his wife with new retirement Army ID cards. Goldfarb at first insisted that they make him lieutenant colonel rather than captain, since his cover story was that he had retired from the military after a lifetime of service, and it would look more logical, given his age. This request was d.o.a., since Shur wasn't going to pass out any bars above captain. We agreed that also that Goldfarb would be protected when he returned to New York to litigate a couple of civil suits in which he and his family were plaintiffs (ordinarily protection extended only to criminal prosecution of federal cases). The Marshals Service set up a post office box for mail transfer, so Goldfarb would receive his dividend checks. We also handled the conversion of his Blue Cross Blue Shield medical coverage to ensure continuity of service under his new alias, Herman G. Martin. What we refused to do, notwithstanding the fact that he was adamant to the end, was to get his wife, Arlene, a teaching job.

The Marshals Service moved Herman and Arlene to San Diego, where he continued his insurance business. Before his death in 1990, he got tagged for a murder. He had apparently coerced one of his employees to pistol-whip a wealthy attorney, Richard Crake, whom Goldfarb contended owed him $100,000. The lawyer died as a result of the beating. In 1982 Goldfarb caught a sentence of sixteen years, but his conviction was reversed on appeal in 1987 because the prosecutor had intimidated witnesses by arresting the first defense witness prior to the trial.

Another witness who complained about his treatment in the program was someone who'd been renamed Jody Alston. He colorfully described his treatment to anyone who would listen as "that afforded to a bastard child of Uncle Sam." Alston was a participant in an auto-theft ring in Ohio when he was busted. He and his wife had owned a customized-van business for sports vehicles and special vans for the handicapped. He began selling stolen cars and trucks through his van business. In June 1978 he was arrested driving a stolen Lincoln Continental. He decided to be a talker rather than a convict, agreeing to work undercover for the FBI agents who had cracked the ring. He avoided prosecution when his testimony sent six ringleaders to jail, and he was given a new identity. He complained that the FBI had promised him a lot but delivered very little.

Alston's dissatisfaction came to a head through a self-initiated interview with the *Dallas Morning News*. The article outlined what was a constant problem with wives of informants: married for six years, his wife was depressed by the reversal of fortune from high living to hiding out on a modest government stipend. She wanted a family but did not want to bring a child into this covert world. I had grown to admire many of these women, who seemed to suffered more than their husbands. Alston's wife had apparently seen a *60 Minutes* piece about the Witness Protection Program the night before she was to enter it, and some of the show was unflattering. Her husband told me she cried all night.

Mrs. Alston, now moved to another location, told the *Dallas Morning News* reporter in her previous city that the only thing she liked about the program was getting rid of the names, Ralph and Rita, that they were given at birth. Jody had once told me, "Ralph was the name of idiots—it's as bad as being Harold," so I chuckled when I saw this in print. They had picked each other's first name and agreed on Alston as the surname, since it put them near the top in alphabetical listings.

For me the article was a confirmation of some bad realities, since it stated that Jody Alston had been coached by the FBI as to what to say to get into the Witness Protection Program. The FBI had trained him to record the theft ring surreptitiously, and he had applied the same skills to his handlers. It was an eye-opener. I took disciplinary action against a marshal who was on tape telling him to earn money under the table to get his life started again. He had also recorded a marshal complaining that he didn't get along with a black administrator in the U.S. Marshals Service because of his color! The PR for the program took a broadside from the article.

Alston claimed that he had been shot in the leg because of a marshal's ineptitude. His version of the story was that there was a considerable amount of marijuana sold and traded in the stereo store where Alston was then working. The marshal came to the store to drop off the last payment under Alston's Witness Protection Program contract. Alston was fired shortly after the marshal's visit and, he said, his vehicle's brake lines were cut; he believed it was because the marshal had made him look like a paid informant. Yet the marshal had done nothing about the marijuana precisely because he had not wanted to tip his hand as to the fact that he was a law enforcement officer. Alston later took a small-caliber bullet in the right leg just above the knee and claimed he had been plugged because of the marshal's visit to the store. The Dallas police asked him to take a polygraph test. Both they and I were skeptical of his story particularly after he refused to take the test.

Another of Alston's criticisms was on target, however, and that was that the good guys sometimes overpromised. There was a tendency of some in law enforcement to drop an informant like a hot potato after the convictions were made, as I had observed personally.

Yet another guy with a penchant for complaining to the media about his treatment in the program was John Massaro. Everything went pretty smoothly during the time he was under wraps, but he personified the down-the-road problems. These were situations that arose when informants became unemployed or had to return to the neighborhoods where they had lived of crime.

In Massaro's case, his grandfather had died in New Jersey, and Massaro wanted to go to the funeral. His problem was that he had testified against three gangland figures in Newark, New Jersey, only three years prior to the death. Headquarters refused to pay for a detail to accompany him, so he went on his own. He stayed around because he had no money—he'd been chronically unemployed since Uncle Sam's dime had run out.

One day he read a newspaper column about another protected witness, Thomas Gascoyne, a former master burglar, whom Massaro perceived was living the life of Riley. Apparently, Gascoyne had cut a better deal with the government. Massaro's bitterness wasn't helped by the fact that he was spotted by a confederate of the three loan-sharking guys he had testified against. The government gave him two weeks of protection before cutting him loose again. After being snubbed by the program for future assistance, he went to the *Buffalo Courier Express*, which wrote a multipart series about his travails.

He had trained in oil burner maintenance as part of his relocation plan, but he hated it and quit. He dabbled in petty crimes to make ends meet. As his plight gained some notoriety, Massaro decided to sue the government, but settled the lawsuit cheaply: $1,000, a plane ticket to Houston, Texas, and help in getting a job when he got there. He signed a release barring him from future services.

I felt he had a legitimate beef. Even something innocuous— like the fact that he was assigned the name John Scott even though he appeared decidedly Italian—was a mistake he was justified in complaining about. I was so overextended that I didn't handle his subsequent relocation, but the guy should have been given a fairer shake. I checked out how he was doing and learned that he was in Texas, working in menial daily-hire jobs.

The core problem was the very structure of the program. By its nature, the Witness Protection Program was designed to be a finite experience with a beginning and an end. The theory was that as more of the bad guys were arrested and imprisoned and as time passed without the informant being found out, then one could gradually reduce oversight and payments. In practice, this did not always work out. The biggest problem was getting the witness to abandon the mindset that he was being pensioned by the government for life. Certainly, relocation was based primarily on risk assessment, but another factor was employment, so that the witness could get off the dole.

Many of the hoods who came through the system were "button men"—low-ranking thieves or scammers. If a witness had a skill, the marshal had to secure a job for him using that skills but not in the exact occupation itself, so that he couldn't be traced. Uncle Sam paid for job training, but don't think this was a piece of cake. Most of these guys didn't want an average stiff's job. Lack of interest in earning an honest buck had propelled them into a life of crime in the first place. Even if they did want to work, if they had rubbed out people for a living, how was I supposed to get them excited about flipping hamburgers at McDonald's? Fortunately, we had liaisons with about one hundred corporations where the CEOs had agreed to hire program graduates. We'd brief the owner on what the guy did and on how to protect his business. More often than not, they took the risk and hired the felon. One reason CEOs participated was that the program had just a 20 percent recidivism rate—much better than the odds with inmates coming out of penal institutions.

A written contract was eventually implemented by the program, specifying the actual length of the terms of protection and payments to the witness, so we could prevent the "he promised this" syndrome.

Sometimes the informants were shortchanged simply because the program was taking in more people than could be processed in a timely manner. One guy who got the short end of the stick was Raymond Freda. His wife and children languished for thirteen weeks in a motel. He was in jail and was scheduled to be an informant to crack a drug ring. The Justice Department had told Freda that their home would be sold, with the proceeds being turned over to the family. The Fredas also owned a business that was supposed to be sold in a timely manner. Both sales dragged on without any resolution. The truck they had left behind had $2,000 worth of tools in it when it was repossessed. Their store was foreclosed by the landlord for nonpayment of rent, and Freda forfeited about $19,000 he had invested in the premises.

I waited more than nine hours with Mrs. Freda for the movers to come for their furniture, but they were no-shows, and nobody could explain why they were missing in action. They came later, when no marshals were around, and Freda claimed that $4,500 had gone missing and that the movers had consumed all his whiskey.

The Fredas put in an insurance claim, but they had no receipts from the moving company because a marshal had told them to destroy all documents with their names on them. The final straw was that the marshal in charge boarded the family's two dogs in a veterinary hospital and forgot about them; the dogs were subsequently gassed as strays. I went to bat for the Fredas when all of this came to my attention, and the government eventually made restitution for all losses, including the two pooches.

As the program became more successful in attracting participants, more of these slipups occurred. Informants sometimes had bogus complaints in order to squeeze more money out of Uncle Sugar and to prolong protection. One person who was a master of extending the terms and money was Jimmy "the Weasel" Fratianno. He had supposedly earned his nickname by outrunning patrolmen on the streets in his native Cleveland.

Fratiano became a guest of the government in 1978 after he thought there was a contract out on his life. A risk assessment kept him on the outside as an informant. He had risen through the ranks to become acting boss of the Los Angeles crime family and was privy to information exchanged at the highest levels of organized crime throughout the country. Fratianno claimed he knew that Florida crime boss Santo Trafficante, Jr., was going to do a favor for the CIA by killing Fidel Castro as part of Operation Mongoose. Fratianno formally entered the program for protection in 1981 when he felt he was pushing his luck as an informant on the inside.

Jimmy Fratianno was a Mafia hit man who had committed or engineered eleven murders. One famous matter that he was involved in was the murder of the Two Tonys—Tony Brancato and Tony Trombino. They were particularly vicious guys who didn't care what enemies they made, not even the hand that fed them, mobster Mickey Cohen. The Two Tonys had robbed the Flamingo Hotel in Las Vegas, a real no-no at the time, given its mob connections. Fratianno was recruited to bump them off.

Fratianno conned the men into thinking that they were going to knock over a high-stakes poker game. The two men picked up Jimmy and another hood on Hollywood Boulevard in Los Angeles. Fratianno climbed into the backseat and promptly emptied his pistol into the brains of both guys. He then got out of the car, took a shower, and headed out for a night of club-hopping. Although he was booked for the murders, the case fell apart. A waitress had vouched that Jimmy was at the Five O'Clock Club all night. She later retracted her alibi. By the time the trial was scheduled, she had recanted again, saying that Jimmy was there but that two detectives had burned her with cigarettes to make her give false information against him. When Fratianno entered the program he acknowledged that he was the hit man after all, but by that time he had immunity.

With immunity as his shield, Fratianno implicated the Mafia boss of all Mafia bosses, Carlo Gambino of New York, and underbosses Gregory de Palma and Thomas Marson. During the celebrated fraud and obstruction-of-justice case in the operations of the Westchester Premier Theater in Westchester County, New York, a photograph of the defendants and Fratianno with Frank Sinatra and a brown paper bag with $20,000 in it was central to the prosecution's case. The defendants were accused of skimming hundreds of thousands of dollars from concessions and ticket revenues and defrauding the theater's investors. It was a typical bust-out scheme in which Gambino and Company sucked dry every legitimate dollar invested or earned until the theater was teetering on bankruptcy. The photograph was apparently taken when Frank Sinatra performed at the theater for a reported $800,000 (in 1976 dollars) for a weeklong performance. Sinatra always attracted sellout crowds, so the mob wanted him to perform as often as possible to entice investors to throw more money into the pot. In the picture, Sinatra's arm was draped around two mob guys, and Gambino was grinning. While Fratianno would implicate Sinatra in organized crime capers, the only nefarious act traced to Sinatra was his bad taste in friends.

Jimmy Fratianno claimed that Sinatra was conned by him into working for free at the Theater on another occasion. As he told it, Fratianno knew that Sinatra wanted to be inducted into an exclusive social order, the Knights of Malta. He also promised Sinatra that he'd get him the Maltese Cross, an honor that had been bestowed only seven hundred times in the order's thousand-year history. A dubious ceremony was held by a Hungarian named Ivan Markovics, who said he was a high-ranking Knight of Malta, and Sinatra got his cross. Fratianno then confided in Sinatra that the Knights had fallen on bad times financially and suggested a benefit concert. Sinatra agreed to perform for free at—where else?—the Westchester Theater, where the mob made 100 percent profit from the charitable event. Fratianno's nickname "Weasel" took on a new meaning.

Fratianno allegedly promised Sinatra that he'd repay him for his kindness. In the biography written by Ovid Demaris, *The Last Mafioso* (1985),[1] Fratianno claimed that Sinatra allegedly wanted a former bodyguard, Andy "Banjo" Celentano, roughed up because Banjo was going to pen a tell-all story about Ol' Blue Eyes and needed some encouragement to cancel his plans. Fratianno promised to take care of it. In one trial Fratianno recounted this story and claimed his leg-breakers couldn't find the guy, so he couldn't keep his word. As for the brown paper bag

---

1. Ovid Demaris, *The Last Mafioso: The Treacherous World of Jimmy Fratianno* (New York: Times Books, 1981).

with the twenty gees, the Weasel said it was the proverbial "bag money" for the proceeds from the evening when Sinatra sang.

In a series of other trials, Fratianno's testimony convicted Frank "Funzi" Tieri, Carmine "Junior" Persico, and Dominic Brooklier, all of whom were reportedly mob bosses. Anthony "Fat Tony" Salerno was also convicted of fixing the elections of Teamsters Union presidents Roy Williams and Jackie Presser. There's no question that Fratianno provided valuable information to the government.

In 1987, however, the Marshals Service decided to cut off Fratianno's living allowance. Fratianno squealed louder than he had against any mobster—he went to the media. Then Justice Department spokesman John Russell stated that the Witness Protection Program "was never intended to be a retirement plan for former mobsters." He added that Mr. Fratianno was able to take care of his own finances. That assessment was true.

Fratianno received a stipend of $25,000 a year in 1976 dollars at government expense. He received free medical and dental insurance for himself and his family, plus rent and all utilities. He wanted to move a lot, because he'd become squirrelly about being a target. Despite his concern about getting hit, he made frequent appearances in TV crime documentaries and even appeared on *60 Minutes* to promote two books about his life as a hit man. Besides receiving hefty fees for his documentary work, he raked in cash from royalties on his book and appeared as a paid expert in civil cases. He was able to own a condominium and another $190,000 beach condo somewhere in Texas. Relationships began to sour between Fratianno and the government when the Justice Department refused to pay for the cleaning and reglazing of his wife's mink. In all, Fratianno received around $1.1 million.

In December 1987 Fratianno met with a reporter from *People* magazine to protest the planned cessation of his subsidy. He complained that he had gone through nine cars because he was afraid that an enemy would "make" his wheels. When the reporter pointed out that he was wearing a diamond, he told her that his two rings had been in the family for years. One was 2.5 carats and the other was 1.5, but, he explained, he "bought them cheap." The female reporter, whom he constantly called "Honey," then asked him why taxpayers should pay money to keep up the lifestyle of an admitted killer. He responded that he had never killed an innocent person; they were all gangsters.[2]

The Justice Department protected Fratianno until he decided to move back to his old haunts. He explained that he was seventy-four and had to go where he knew people. The money faucet was turned off, Tony went back to where he knew people, and he died a natural death as a very rich man.

2. *People* magazine, December 31, 1987, 40.

21

MANAGEMENT TENSIONS

In case it seems that everybody in Witness Protection is a gangster or perpetrator, let me tell you that we sometimes protect the not-so-guilty, too. In addition to the occasional innocent witness, there are folks who aren't 100 percent dirty—rather they just have a few smudges. Take the case of Paul Rego.

In his late forties this talented engineer was a smashing success. His lucrative engineering company was raking in contracts. He lived in a mansion in the swank neighborhood of Oldwick, New Jersey, with his wife, three youngest children, and eight dogs. He owned five automobiles, a helicopter, and a motor launch.

Rego and his wife were British. Their children went to the finest schools: the Christian Brothers at the LaSalle Military Academy in Oakdale on Long Island taught the two boys, and the teenage daughter attended the School of the Holy Child in Suffern, New York, a stone's throw away from West Point. Their oldest child, a daughter, was married and living in Highbridge, New Jersey. Rego seemed to have a perfect life.

Rego's dream turned into a nightmare one morning, however, shortly after he landed a Newark city contract. Two hoods who represented Anthony "Tony Boy" Boiardo stopped by his office to pick up a 10 percent kickback for the award of the contract. Rego believed that he had gotten the contract on his own merit. He realized that Tony Boy was the son of Ruggiero "Richie the Boot" Boiardo, a ruthless Genovese capo, but he refused to pay. The thugs forced him into a car and drove him to Boiardo's family estate. The Boot lived in a baronial setting—a huge stone mansion, several smaller houses, an aviary, a deer park, a greenhouse, two pools, and a life-sized statue of Boiardo on horseback, flanked by busts of his relatives. An iron gate swung closed as Rego was driven toward the mansion. Tony Boy got his money after threatening to break both of Rego's legs with a baseball bat and kill Rego's family if he squealed. As Rego was about to learn, a yes once is a yes forever when it comes to the mob.

Soon more and more city contracts came Rego's way. The Boiardos were bribing Newark city officials under the direction of Mayor Hugh Addonizio to hire Rego's firm. After skimming their tithe from the top, the mob recruited Rego as a bagman to collect kickbacks from other contractors. He got deeper and deeper into the mob's pocket, until he couldn't stand it anymore. Rego's creative bookkeeping to mask the kickbacks had brought the IRS snooping around. He decided to extricate himself and met with Gerald Shur, an assistant U.S. attorney. After Shur vetted his offer and whom he could implicate, the marshals were summoned to protect Rego and his family.

Paul Rego's primary threats were the Boiardo Cosa Nostra family, a Newark council member, Calvin West, and the mayor. The marshals knew that a fourth significant threat came from Tony LaMorte, executive director of the Newark Utilities Authority.

At the initial interview Paul Rego stated that on a prior occasion, when he had been seen in the company of a prosecutor, he returned to his car and found a card on the front window: "This could have been a bomb—watch your mouth." The note was followed up by a phone call telling him to be careful. "You have a pretty daughter," the voice warned. "Suffering isn't too far."

We tried to assess the threats to the rest of his family. Rego recounted that his son's attendance at the military academy was common knowledge. Accordingly, I knew that all his children would require a detail. The least in danger, Mr. Rego opined, was his married daughter, but I decided to provide a discreet watch.

Paul Rego was a little guy. The more agitated he was, the more he fiddled with his gray goatee and eyeballed his very petite wife for affirmation.

Deputy Marshal Hugh McDonald, from my office, was to be the point man. The IRS saw an opportunity to prosecute income-tax evasion, so that department assigned Special Agents Gardener and Miller from the Newark office. Because the investigation involved both criminal and political leaders in the State of New Jersey, no local, county, or state police would be utilized in the personal-security mission. In fact, although the IRS agents said they knew of no corrupt elements in the local U.S. Marshals office, they nonetheless requested and received marshals from outside the state to guard the Regos. Within two days, all security was in place for the family.

Rego's mansion was a fortress with one exit, so we decided to guard him and his wife there, with other bodyguards for the children. The entire household's butlers and maids were background-checked, and deputies protected the family round the clock. Cameras were installed, and the marshals patrolled the property using Rego's snowmobiles in winter.

Rego was debriefed every day. The inevitable indictments were soon to be issued, and then Rego decided to sell his house. Logistically, this was a new wrinkle for the service. We had to vet all wannabe purchasers, prescreening them to make sure they were actually able to buy the house. A marshal posing as a salesperson would accompany the sales agent, so nothing could be planted on-site. Other agents would be working around the house, and the family wouldn't be there when a prospect came through. Fortunately, the house sold rapidly, and it was time to relocate. However, the Regos had tens of thousands of dollars-worth of antiques that they wanted us to move. The antiques were crated up and shipped to a military base until a final destination was selected after the trials.

During this time I got in trouble with my superiors. There was a reported flu epidemic about to hit, so I had authorized the Rego family and the marshals guarding them to get flu shots. Fifteen people were inoculated, including me, at five dollars apiece. I was berated over this seventy-five-dollar "unauthorized" expenditure by the newly created inspector's office in the marshal's service. Because of the burgeoning of the program, we had many irons in the fire, and bad things had happened—like marshals' guns being stolen by protected witnesses—in other details, but my units were flawless, so I was very surprised that such a commonsense expense had drawn the wrath of the inspector, Jim Gardiner. Without explanation I was pulled off the Rego detail and sent back to Providence to cool my heels; I had nothing to do. Finally, I was summoned to D.C. I was told to pack for three days, so I went there very happy that I was going to be assigned a job again.

"What's going on, guys?" I asked, as I spotted, Reis Kash, and Jim Gardiner. Kash snubbed me with a curt, "We won't be talking until after you finish with Inspector Gardiner," and exited the room. Gardiner then Mirandized me. I was thinking, *What's all this shit?* After a ration of bull for about an hour while a stenographer typed away, Gardiner presented me with a $500 invoice. "We told you after the flu shot incident to get authorization," he sneered, "but look at this. You disobeyed orders." He threw the invoice on the desk. I looked at it. "What's it for?" I asked.

"You tell me, Partington. What the hell you doing, ordering things without permission?"

I looked again at this invoice. I had never authorized it. The name of the marshal who did, J. Butler, was at the bottom.

"Ya got the wrong guy," I scowled back. I thumped the invoice on the table and pointed to Butler's name. Gardiner's face drained. He summoned Reis and pointed out the problem.

I was livid. I had poured my heart and soul into every assignment. We had never had a hitch, and here I was, being upbraided for nothing and sitting out my duties while they fiddled around trying to justify their inspector jobs. I always brought my battered briefcase when I went to meetings. I was so angry at this penny-ante stuff that I kicked it across the room. We stood in silence.

"Since you've got nothing else to say, I'm outta here," I announced and left.

Within twenty-four hours I was called to handle a potentially botched job. Ten prisoners incarcerated in a federal prison claimed to have overheard the plotting of a big safe job and demanded protection. Some higher-up granted their request. The reality was that it was a planned escape. The ten would be taken outside the prison walls and hoped to overpower the marshals once outside. The plot was foiled. I was glad to be back in the swing again.

Paul Rego was living in hotels and being shunted from place to place every two or three days, now that indictments had been announced. After several months, Mayor Addonizio, Tony Boy Boiardo, and thirteen city officials and contractors were convicted of corruption charges and income-tax evasion. A Newark judge, James Del Mauro, was also brought down. The trial proved that everything was for sale at City Hall.

Paul Rego was relocated, and as far as I know, he made a legitimate living as an engineer under his assumed name. The Boiardo crime family didn't fare as well. The Boot's bodyguard was found dead in the trunk of a car in May 1973. The bodyguard, Angelo Chieppa, apparently met his fate for skimming off the top at a casino owned by the mob boss in Antigua.

Of all the people I had to protect, Paul Rego stands out in my mind. He had a rocky and dangerous road to travel but he never complained. His wife was a stalwart. Many a time she reminded me of my own sweet wife, who backed me up through thick and thin. I figured he was a lucky man, just like I was.

22

RELAPSE

The program's clients are hardly angels. About 97 percent of protected witnesses are convicted felons, and the pressure to relocate witnesses is often because of death threats. In the heat of an investigation, prosecutors push the Marshals Service to protect their star witnesses. As Rudy Giuliani, assistant U.S. attorney from 1970 to 1975, observed to a Senate committee, "It's a program by definition that has inherent problems. You're taking into the program a group of people who are criminals testifying against other criminals, and people with behavior problems."[1] Many witnesses eventually require little supervision after the threats against them abate once the organized-crime enterprise is dismantled. While many of the protected witnesses and families have done well or have even prospered, roughly 20 percent returned to crime, and some of those committed murders. These were considered the main exhibits of what was wrong with the program from the public's point of view.

When crimes were committed by Witness Protection Program graduates, I'm sure there was some dogging of the

---

1. Senate Permanent Subcommittee on Investigations into the Witness Protection Program, 1980.

investigations by the embarrassed service, but most of the time this was inadvertent: because the mob had been successful in compromising law enforcement, witnesses identities were shared only on a need-to-know basis therefore, the very same obstacles that prevented the bad guys discovering the whereabouts of the stoolies also thwarted police inquiries as well.

The first murder by a program participant during my watch was committed on April 21, 1976. Two aspiring musicians and best buddies, Leslie Michael Nellis, twenty-two, and Charles Murphy, twenty, were shot to death gangland-style at the Treetops Apartments in New Albany, Indiana. The slaying was a case where the lack of knowledge about the perpetrator might have contributed to the murders. Earlier, the protected witness, who'd been renamed Frank Bellman, was suspected of a burglary, but when his scrubbed record came up, it showed no criminal past; the authorities let him walk.

Bellman was really a high-echelon dope dealer named Frank Bova. He was employed as a security chief at an apartment complex where the two young men worked as waiters. They were nabbed for the burglary and were reportedly about to turn in Bellman as the mastermind, but he got wind of it and shot them both several times in the head. The police probably would not have overlooked Bellman if they had known his past. A talkative FBI agent finally disclosed who Bellman really was; his record included a murder of a dope dealer before his entrance into the program. He was subsequently arrested and convicted for the killings.

On October 22, 1977, suspected big-time cocaine smuggler, Steven Bovan, was shot nine times and left on the tony Newport Beach in California. Two relocated witnesses, Jerry Flori and Raymond Jesco, and the son of Anthony Marone, Jr., another relocated witness, were convicted. The men found each other in close proximity, revealed their pasts to each other, and set up their own Mafia-style gang involved in drugs, extortion, and murder.

On November 6, 1981, Brian Casey, twenty-seven, was shot four times outside an Oklahoma Veterans of Foreign Wars dance hall. Protected witness Marcus Love was charged with second-degree murder. He had come into the program while I was in charge. Love was at a dance with his wife when he got involved in an argument with Casey. He pulled a pistol from his wife's purse and ended the argument by plugging Casey, a factory worker. Love was the second witness to be moved into the county, and the local police were livid that their burg had become a dumping ground.

Earl Cassell, who had a previous record for assaulting a police officer with a firearm, was taken into the program in 1977. Two years later, armed with a new name and another gun, he shot a Pascagoula, Mississippi, clerk in the head eleven times. The Justice Department stonewalled the investigation. Cassell ended up serving time for manslaughter, but if the local police had had access to his record, as a career criminal he would have been jailed for life without parole.

The worst graduate by far was Marion Albert Pruett, who killed at least five people before being captured and executed. In 1979 Pruett was given $800 per month for a year and a new name, Charles Sonny Pearson, upon release from a twenty-three-year sentence for bank robbery; he was placed in the Witness Protection Program after testifying against a fellow inmate who was convicted of killing another prisoner in an Atlanta, Georgia, federal prison. After he was caught in a series of murders, Pruett acknowledged that he had murdered the inmate himself.

In April 1981, Pruett walked into a police station in New Mexico to report that somebody had killed his wife, Pamela Sue Carnuteson. The authorities found her body beaten with a hammer and burned with gasoline. While the police were investigating, Pruett fled, embarking upon a cross-country spree of armed robberies, abductions, and murder. Among his most savage attacks was the abduction and murder of Peggy Lowe, a savings and loan officer in Jackson, Mississippi, and mother of two. He would later lead authorities to the body, which he had dumped in a wooded area in Alabama. In separate robberies, Pruett shot in the head two young 7-Eleven store clerks who were earning money for their college tuitions.

On October 11, 1981, Pruett arrived in Fort Smith, Arkansas, and scouted the city for a place to commit yet another robbery. Most establishments were closed on that Sunday, so he parked at a place known as Horseshoe Bend. There he injected himself with cocaine and consumed whiskey for several hours. Sometime after midnight, he later said, he remembered that he had passed a Convenience Corner grocery store during a previous trip to the town. He drove over there, peeked in the window, and saw Bobbie Jean Robertson, age thirty, working the night shift. As he would later confess, "I pulled in and was going to get gas and I seen that there was a girl working there by herself and I said, well, hell, I think I'll just rob her and kill her, so that's what I done."

According to his later confession, he then ordered her to place the money from the cash register into a paper bag. She complied. He then ordered her into his car and drove her to the secluded Arkansas wooded area of Horseshoe Bend, telling her along the way that if she cooperated he'd let her go. Upon arrival, he ordered her out of the car, and she quickly began to walk away. She paused and asked for her purse. Pruett raised his gun and shot her. The first shot hit her upper-left thigh, fracturing the femur. She struggled to run away. Pruett let off another bullet, which ripped her right shoulder, and she fell to the ground. Pruett got out of the car, walked up to her, and pressed the muzzle of the revolver against her left temple. The third shot killed her. He returned to the car with the purse and the $165 loot from the robbery. The police discovered her body the next day.

Five days later Pruett was stopped for speeding by a Texas police officer who spotted the holster carrying the weapon protruding from the front seat. The officer promptly arrested Pruett, who subsequently gave detailed confessions of his crimes, except for Mrs. Robertson. He received consecutive life sentences for the other murders. The Robertson trial was the one used to secure a death penalty. Various technicalities about the trial kept the case kicking around for years. Pruett delivered his own closing argument, but the jury was not impressed; they found him guilty and directed that he be electrocuted.

Pruett was subsequently shipped to New Mexico for trial in the murder of his wife and he was again found guilty. Then governor Bill Clinton sought and received the extradition of Pruett back to Arkansas for the implementation of the death penalty. Execution was scheduled for April 7, 1988, but the district court granted a stay of execution three days before Pruett's date with the chair. Subsequent court proceedings extended over nine years; at one point the court vacated the conviction for Mrs. Robertson's murder and ordered Arkansas to release Pruett or retry him within 120 days. The grounds for reversal were pretrial publicity and the admission of improper testimony from a witness who had been hypnotized during the penalty phase, which was viewed by the court as influencing the death penalty decision. The State of Arkansas appealed the decision. The Appellate Court rejected the argument that pretrial publicity had tainted the proceedings. The hypnosis argument was also rejected. On April 13, 1999, Pruett was executed by lethal injection, rather than electrocution, because Arkansas had changed its execution method in the interim. Pruett showed no remorse; he relished his self-imposed epithet of mad-dog killer.

Another near-fatality caused by Pruett was the potential death of the Witness Protection Program. In the end, however, Pruett's case resulted in needed reform regarding background checks on applicants and caps on the number of entrants. Although I didn't have direct contact with Pruett, I know we marshals all felt in some measure that we were to blame and should have been more circumspect in the supervision aspect of his program. Of course, the Justice Department was the ultimate boss, both in the enrollment of the witness and in the level of supervision, so I'm not sure what I might have accomplished had I been more involved. I did appear on *The Phil Donahue Show* to appeal for more transparency with local law enforcement when an inquiry is made following an arrest for a serious investigation or prosecution.

This black eye to the program was followed by John Sliker, whose name is dead-on in describing the kind of slick guy he was. After testifying in a counterfeit and loan-shark trial that netted Uncle Sam $600,000 illegally deposited in a Caribbean tax shelter, he was deposited in Albuquerque, New Mexico. The local authorities had no idea that he was the same guy awaiting trial for defrauding Pennsylvania residents of half a million dollars. He promptly relieved local Albuquerque of another $400,000. After making bail, he skipped to Canada, where he was eventually apprehended.

One mob witness whom I protected embarrassed me bigtime. Frank DeLeo showed up in California as a strong-arm for some self-proclaimed the Hare Krishnas. Somehow he got together with previously relocated witnesses, all of whom were in different cities, to form a new gang while they were all still on the public dole. Together they weaseled themselves into a Hare Krishna enterprise (later disavowed by Krishna leadership) known as Prasadam Distributors International Inc.

On the surface the company was marketing "bionic bits," a health-food cookie, along with a beverage called Hiku Hawaiian Honey Nectar. The real business of Prasadam, however, was money-laundering drug proceeds by investing in so-called legitimate companies. Eventually, the authorities caught on to the true nature of the transactions, as did the sect followers. The latter were incensed. For the believer, eating *prasadam*—food prepared for and offered to Krishna with love and devotion—was a spiritual exercise; Krishna imparted a spiritual value to the sanctified offering. For the devotees, the heroin smuggling and money-laundering constituted a violation of their religion bordering on sacrilege. DeLeo and his fellow musclemen were eventually arrested and jailed for the murder of competitors.

Ultimately, these problems involving relocated witnesses gone bad came to the attention of politicians, and hearings were held to reevaluate the efficacy of the Witness Protection Program. My bosses were summoned, and I volunteered to appear, much to their chagrin. I had a lot to say, particularly since I felt they would sugarcoat the shortcomings of the program.

23

REFORM

Because of the deterioration of the Witness Protection Program, in December 1980 I asked for and was granted a time slot to appear before the Senate Permanent Subcommittee on Investigations, headed by Senator Sam Nunn, concerning the program.

I had previously, answered all questions truthfully before another investigative Senate panel in 1978. Then–U.S. Senator James Abourezk, who was conducting those hearings, addressed me. He said that some of his colleagues had privately informed the Senate staff that "if you testify fully and completely before this committee, it will virtually end your career with the Marshals Service." I replied that I had received no direct threats so far and added, "It is a very awkward position to be in. I started with the program. It's a personal thing. I watched it grow."

In the end, I shrugged off the downside of his comment, knowing full well that retribution would happen. Sure enough, the Marshals Service tried to bag me again for unexplained "huge" expenses shortly after my testimony. One of the items in question was a fuel pump for the burner of a protected witness who had paid for the item himself, and the other was a thirty-dollar expenditure for heating oil, which I paid for out of my own pocket. The furnace had given out because it had no oil, and I knew the oilman, who delivered the items for me over a holiday. I had the receipt showing that I had paid the bill myself. When no reimbursement vouchers for the items were located, the matter was dropped. I regarded this nit-picking incident, however, as a shot across the bow. A reassignment to a desk job in Providence that soon followed was I felt, also retribution. I felt bad because I had been able to put out a lot of little fires while I was in the field.

With me stuck at my desk, problems multiplied because of the inexperience of some of the field marshals and certainly because of the desk jockeys in D.C. However, in the Washington bosses' view, my testimony had made them look bad, so they'd rather make sure I didn't know about recurring problems than see me try to improve the program.

Notwithstanding my banishment from the hands-on work in the field, thirty-three of the thirty-five proposals I made at the 1978 hearing were being implemented by the incoming director of the program, Howard Safir. I was pleased to see the month-to-month improvements under his leadership. Safir began slowing the intake, and the higher-ups got more involved. Appropriate training of new marshals was enforced. Safir fought for and got an increase in his budget. Most important was that he required uniform briefing of witnesses so that false promises wouldn't be made, and as I had suggested, only the marshals could now make promises.

When I returned to D.C. in 1980, now as the U.S. marshal for Rhode Island, I still felt that the credentialing of witnesses was running amok and that several other issues hadn't yet been addressed. I also felt that the program should reach out to good citizens who witnessed bad things. Fully 97 percent of the program participants had been involved in crime themselves. As I used to plead (for naught), "There ought to be room for the Billy Grahams, not just the bad guys." The program continued to be understaffed by about 40 percent. We weren't just police-men doing guard duty—we had to be problem solvers and so-cial workers too.

The stage was set for the December 1980 Senate subcom-mittee hearing by a *20/20* segment called "Hostages of Fear." The ABC-TV show explained that it had been a bad summer for protected government witnesses. One had hanged himself out of desperation over not receiving his new credentials, an-other committed suicide before his trial against thirty cohorts in an auto-theft ring, and another witness was returned over his objection to the zone of danger in Bridgeport from whence he came; he killed himself, too. Three major drug trials had to be postponed because the star witness bolted from the program claiming the marshals had blown his cover.

One witness who really impressed me was Art Rocco Bel-tran, the former number-three guy in California's notorious La Nuestra Familia, a Mexican gang that had its genesis inside prison. He argued for a separate federal wing in a prison for the witnesses who were serving time, since the very families that a witness was testifying against might have members inside the prison.

During the three-day Senate hearing, it was learned that 20 percent of the 3,500 witnesses then in the program were out of work. The Social Security Administration was blamed as the main culprit for obstructing gainful employment by the pro-gram's participants because of the snail-like processing of Social Security cards. That department was also accused of a separate-kingdom mentality and an "I'll do it when I get around to it" attitude. As I pointed out, states had to cooperate in the docu-menting process. Fourteen states refused because of fears that they would be liable for damages if anything went wrong. Dur-ing my testimony I called for a streamlined central unit that would cut through the layers of bureaucracy.

I stressed that many guys just don't know how to live a simple life—they needed to be taught basic skills such as how to pay a bill. I pounded the idea that you cannot breach faith with these witnesses who put their lives on the line nor can you fail to provide the documents they need to live safely: "We become no better than the people they are testifying against. That's how they feel when we let them down. This common respect has to be accorded to the witness." I firmly believe what I said then I always showed respect to the witnesses I lived with or worked with—it's the only way. Nothing will bring about the demise of the Witness Protection Program faster than broken promises to the witnesses.

Shortly after my testimony, I finished my term as the U.S. marshal for Rhode Island and moved on to become police chief in my home town of Cumberland, Rhode Island, and then safety commissioner in Providence. I was no longer privy to the inner workings of the program, except that naturally enough I was attracted to news reports of what was going on with witnesses. Some mistakes were being repeated, but as far as I know, they were aberrations. Maybe the Senate hearings did some good and shored up the professionalism of the service.

24

A SURPRISING REINFORCEMENT

While controversy raged on about the success or lack thereof of the program, several participants surprised me by their defense of how they were treated. Like the proverbial groundhog, they'd emerge momentarily to sing the program's praises and then disappear underground. These guys tended to be realists, as opposed to those who were looking for pie in the sky. Take, for example, Gerard Festa, a.k.a. Chicken Delight. His nickname was a result of his and his wife's running a Chicken Delight franchise in Newark, New Jersey, in the seventies. Members of this midlevel mobster's gang often met at the restaurant. Initially, the name was given to Festa in good fun, but it took on another definition—"stool pigeon"—after he decided to turn state's evidence against his former confreres.

Festa had obviously heard a lot as he dished out chicken dinners, because his testimony resulted in the convictions of thirty-eight organized-crime figures. Many of the crimes, ranging from murder to loan-sharking, had been unsolved until he provided his information. His memory was legendary. He could recite chapter and verse of the smallest detail of jobs he had done or capers he had heard about, including the colors of the walls in the rooms and the exact locations of the rooms in a home he was ripping off.

Festa was locked up on murder charges when I first met him. I felt he was trying to save his own skin after he had spent four months in jail awaiting his trial. He had quite a tale to tell me about how he had tried to get out of the mob for years but they wouldn't let him. "You could go to them and say you are moving to North Dakota and want out. Maybe a week later, . . ." he'd curl his finger around an imaginary trigger and point to his temple. He was visited in jail by the local law enforcement, who worked with the Justice Department to put him in witness protection. The Feds also took a keen interest because for ten years they had been searching for a way to crack the Boiardo crime syndicate and the Joe Paterno mob in New Jersey; Festa was their entrée. Thrown in for good measure would be some potential indictments of corrupt cops and political figures.

The very first time I had to escort Festa to a grand jury, he swore up and down to me during the ride that he decided to be a witness against his confreres for the sake of his kids. "I wanted to get out but I couldn't," he'd complain. When a relative who was also in the mob visited Festa's sixteen-year-old daughter near her school, warning her to convey to her father that the mob knew about his potential cooperation with authorities, he decided he had to get out of his association immediately.

Finding a safe haven for him and his family wasn't easy. He stood six feet five inches tall in bare feet, so he was easily recognizable. I housed him in a series of incarceration settings for short bursts of time. Festa had so many grand jury appearances and subsequent trials that we had to move his family a lot as well. His wife, Rose, and the kids were frequently uprooted during the two years he spent testifying. He had a very cute daughter, Cindy Jean, who was nineteen when the family came under protection. She was a near recluse because she was ashamed to let potential boyfriends know too much about her. Gerard and his wife seemed genuinely pained that his life of crime had caused such dislocation for them. They had two other daughters and two small sons. His sixty-five-year-old father also had to be protected. Rose had a minor heart problem, and one of the daughters had a serious illness, so medical records for them had to be carefully concocted for their post-relocation life.

Festa told me that he had stumbled into a life of crime. In his midtwenties he started swindling old ladies on phony roof repairs. He was an inveterate gambler and was soon borrowing from loan sharks to support his pony habit. "I lost easily over a million dollars," he'd shrug. He had gotten addicted to gambling after mob associates took him to a track, and he won $1,000 on a fixed race. This turned out to what his appetite for betting on the ponies since he wasn't privy to inside information thereafter, but he was hooked. To pay his debts to the loan sharks, he did favors for them, including house burglaries, armed robberies, and, of course, all the chicken they could eat.

His wife was not an innocent spouse. She had been a minor participant in an $80,000 jewelry theft and fencing operation. The big fish she and her husband would testify against was Frank "the Bear" Basto, an associate of Joseph Paterno, a capo in the Gambino family. A whole coterie of crime-family members would bite the dust, since Festa had firsthand knowledge of beatings that were administered to victims of loan-sharking and as a participant in burglaries. To my knowledge no cops or politicians were scored, despite earlier promise, but Festa's testimony nailed enough mobsters that the foundation of these crime syndicates was shaken.

After their permanent relocation (Festa was never tried on the murder charge for which he was in prison), I was surprised one day to pick up the New York *Daily News* and see Festa's comments in print. He had surfaced to state that his life underground wasn't that bad. He went on to say that he was giving an exclusive to the reporter because "I can't sit back and see individuals take pot shots at the program." He rapped rhapsodically about how the program is the strongest thing the government has going against organized crime and that it got mobsters shaking. He credited it for saving the rest of his life! How did I take his remarks? Unabashedly, let me say—back in those trying days I'd take the praise wherever I could find it!

25

REFLECTIONS

Police officers call each other "brother" (or "sister," as the case may be). The title is rooted in respect. Everybody is a flawed human being, but police officers and other law enforcement generally try to do the right thing. Despite the problems in the Connolly/Bulger caper in Boston, most Fibbies try to get it right, and to be fair, it was a group of them who forced open the truth behind the Bulger affair. More often than not I experienced dedication and a willingness to put their lives on the line from those whose duty it was to protect and to serve.

My experience in the Witness Protection Program gave me an unparalleled opportunity to evaluate human beings. The witnesses were ice-cold killers; as con men, they had no peer. I also observed, however, that these bad guys had a good side. Their word was their bond. They were exemplary parents in many ways. In fact, they were "brothers" of another ilk. The witnesses put away a lot of scourges on our society through testimony that took courage, and that wasn't diminished in my view by their having few options if they wanted to get out of a life of crime.

I felt they had my back, too, when I'd escort them through zones of danger for their testimony. Certainly they were protecting themselves, but they were also making sure I didn't catch a bullet.

During my time with the U.S. Marshals Service, I met consummate professionals on the law enforcement side: guys like Bud Warren and Bud McPherson, who were professional from tip to toe; prosecutors such as O'Neil, Giuliani, O'Sullivan, and a host of others, who were top-notch; and my marshal teammates, who were gutsy guys.

But just as bad guys are sometimes good, good guys can be also be bad. The Boston FBI office is Exhibit A of that reality. For me, the most disappointing element of good guys acting bad was the failure of higher-ups in the Justice Department to live up to promises made to the protected witnesses. Some of the witnesses would rightly complain that they were shunted aside once their testimony was given and another reputation made for somebody in law enforcement. All I could say was, "I hear ya." I was a constant thorn in my superiors' side because I believe that if you give your word, you have to keep it. I was not normally a guy to go public, so the last thing in the world I wanted to do was appear not once but twice before a Senate committee. I did so because I saw it as a route to fix and enhance the program. I did see improvements during my tenure—but promises should be held sacrosanct.

Progress must continue. There will always be a need for the Witness Protection Program. The cast of characters may change, and we may now need protection for those who blow the whistle on terrorists. What cannot change is a stand-up program where safety is provided both before and after cooperation, as promised. I feel very strongly that noncriminals are a ripe field for witness protection, since many of them would never contemplate that they could begin all over again if they came forward. I hope this book may motivate some of those people to lobby for the program to be extended to them.

My wife, Helen, passed away on April 21, 2000. By that time her health, which had steadily declined from the end of my service as Rhode Island's U.S. marshal, finally caught up with her. Nobody could ever take her place. I feel overwhelmed sometimes when I think of all the missed times we could have had together and her deep understanding of my job. Never has a husband had such a supportive wife. While I periodically received acknowledgment for my work, she should have received a gold medal. I see Helen as the true patriot who gave endlessly of herself for this to be a better society. I don't have words enough to praise her as she deserves.

I was diagnosed recently with Guillain-Barré, a rare disease and an enemy I never trained for. It started with a bended knee that wouldn't flex. Eventually, I was fully paralyzed and told I would never recover. For a long time I was in this condition but fought back. I played wheelchair hockey after gaining some mobility and eventually got to run around the backyard with my grandchildren, Jonathan and Emily.

Life has been good to me. I've often been asked whether the sacrifice of living with the bad guys was worth it. The answer is an unqualified yes. The program is vital to fighting systemic crime. When I look at my son, Scott, who is now an attorney and probate judge, I realize that he carries the same torch for justice. I would like to think that he got this passion for justice from my wife and me. I am proud to call him Son.

My life was touched by great love. I also witnessed the very worst that human beings have to offer. Protecting the packages, as we euphemistically called our charges, was worth it personally as well for society's sake. I feel it made me stronger, and I'm grateful for the life I've had.

POSTSCRIPT

After a forty-seven-year career in law enforcement, John Partington died on February 10, 2006, of a viral infection following surgery. He was seventy-seven. There was standing room only at his funeral in the Cathedral of Saints Peter and Paul in Providence, Rhode Island, the place to which he was en route with Senator Bobby Kennedy and Judge Raymond Pettine when the Witness Protection Program was born.

ACKNOWLEDGMENTS

Were John Partington still alive, he undoubtedly would want me to thank his wife, Helen, who was the love of his life, and his son, Scott, their pride and joy.

I also want to thank Emma Penick, my wonderful agent; editors extraordinaire Patrick Price and Ed Schlesinger of Gallery Books; Steve Day, who helped with his wonderful anecdotes about John's life; and my mother, Alice Violet, who has been a lifetime mentor to me.

—Arlene Violet